Microwave Cooking · From The Freezer

Litton Microwave Cooking Products, Minneapolis, Minnesota

from Litton

CERTIFIED FOR MICROWAVE COOKING

LITTON Microwave Cooking Products

CREDITS:

Design & Production: Cy DeCosse Creative Department, Inc.
Author: Barbara Methven
Art Director: Jan Huibregtse
Production Coordinators: Julia Slott, Christine Watkins,
 Elizabeth Woods, Bonita Machel
Photographers: Buck Holzemer, Graham Brown, Jill Greer
Food Stylists: Lynn Lohmann, Susan Zechmann
Home Economists: Jill Crum, Peggy Lamb, Kathy Weber,
 Carol Grones
Typesetting: Jennie Smith
Color Separations: Weston Engraving Co., Inc.
Printing: Moebius Printing Co.

This is no ordinary recipe book. It's like a cooking school in your home, ready to answer questions on the spot. Step-by-step photographs show you how to prepare food for microwaving, what to do during cooking, how to tell when the food is done. A new photo technique shows you how foods look during microwaving.

The foods selected for this book are basic in several ways. All microwave well and demonstrate the advantages of microwaving. They are popular foods you prepare frequently, so the book will be useful in day-to-day cooking. Each food illustrates a principle or technique of microwaving which you can apply to similar recipes you find in magazines or other cookbooks.

This book was designed to obtain good results in all brands of ovens. Techniques may vary from the cookbook developed for your oven. If rotating foods is unnecessary in your oven, that technique may be eliminated. All foods are cooked at either High or 50% power (Medium). The Defrost setting on earlier ovens and Simmer setting on current ovens may be used when Medium is called for. This simplifies the choice of settings while you become familiar with the reasons why different foods require different power levels.

Microwaving is easy as well as fast. The skills you develop with this book will help you make full and confident use of your microwave oven.

The Litton Microwave
Cooking Center

Contents

What You Need to Know Before You Start

The microwave oven and the freezer are a natural team. They can add quality, variety and convenience to your meals.

The freezer allows you to take advantage of bargains. You can buy meat in quantity when it is sale-priced. Also, stock up on vegetables in season, when they are at the peak of quality and availability.

The microwave oven defrosts and cooks frozen food rapidly, when you need it. You save time, and the food retains its quality because of shorter defrosting time and less stirring.

With old-fashioned refrigerator defrosting and conventional cooking, you had to remember to remove food from the freezer hours in advance. A turkey might take several days to defrost and hours to cook. Meals were difficult to time because the food might not be defrosted when needed, or it might defrost too soon, and begin to lose the juices which give it flavor and tenderness.

The microwave oven and freezer team is especially convenient for the working person. You can prepare foods in the evening or on weekends when you have the time and store it in the freezer. The microwave oven will speed preparation at the end of a busy day, when time is precious.

Entertaining is easier. Most of the food for a party can be made weeks in advance. With a well-stocked freezer and a microwave oven, you can even invite your guests on the spur of the moment.

Know Your Microwave Oven

Microwave ovens differ in their speed and evenness of cooking. Some heat or defrost more evenly, while others may be faster. House power, which affects the speed of your oven, can vary depending on the time of day. There also may be fluctuations in power due to the season of the year. The directions and recipes in this book provide a time range to allow for these differences.

All Freezers are not Alike

Several types of freezers are available, and their average temperatures differ. Defrosting and storage times are based on a temperature of 0°F.

Separate freezers maintain temperatures of 0°F. or below. The chest style is generally colder than an upright model. The temperature in the freezer section of a double door refrigerator-freezer combination usually ranges from 0° to 5°F. The style may be over, under or side-by-side. The freezer compartment of a single door refrigerator can be as high as 15°F. This temperature and the smaller size make it unsuitable for stocking up for long-term storage.

Temperatures are Important

Starting temperature is an important factor in both microwave cooking and defrosting. You may already know that refrigerated food takes longer to cook than room temperature foods. The same thing is true for frozen foods. Foods at −5° and 5°F. are both frozen, but there is a 10° difference between them which affects the length of time they need to defrost.

In this book, the recommended times for storage and defrosting are based on a freezer at 0°F. An accurate freezer thermometer is the best way of judging the actual temperature of frozen food. If you have a fast microwave oven which cooks food in the minimum time and a freezer which is 5°F. or warmer, defrosting times may be shorter than those given in the directions. If your freezer maintains a temperature below 0°F., the food will last longer, but defrosting times will be longer too.

Freezer Management

Your freezer and the food in it represent an investment. For economy and quality, manage it well. There is no point in operating a freezer if you don't keep food in it, and no point in putting food in it if you don't use it. Frozen foods do not keep indefinitely. They may not spoil if kept longer than the recommended storage time, but flavor and texture will deteriorate.

A good freezer arrangement helps you find foods you want without a lengthy search, and lets you see at a glance what needs to be used or replaced.

Keep it Filled

A full freezer operates more efficiently and economically than one which is half full. There is less empty air to keep chilled and the frozen food helps hold the temperature down. As an average, keep your freezer at least two-thirds full. That allows space for more food if you find a good buy or are preparing food in advance for a party or holiday. If you fish, hunt or grow vegetables, let the freezer get a little less full just before the peak season.

What to Freeze

The best foods to freeze are the ones you like and use frequently. Balance and variety are important, too. Buy only as much of one type of food as you will use within the recommended storage time. Unless you have a large freezer, or a large, beef-eating family, taking advantage of supermarket specials will probably be more economical than buying a side of beef.

How Much to Freeze

When you want to freeze in quantity, the guideline is 2 to 3 pounds of unfrozen food per cubic foot of freezer capacity. If you need to freeze more than that at one time, have the food frozen commercially. You can freeze a single item or a pound or two of food without changing the controls or rearranging the freezer.

How to Organize & Keep Track of Frozen Food

Allocate sections of your freezer to different types of foods, such as uncooked vegetables, meat, poultry or fish, prepared main dishes and desserts.

Use dividers, baskets or shelves, depending on the style of your freezer, to separate the different foods. Keep small items or irregular shapes which don't stack well in an open box, basket or shopping bag to make storage easier.

Keep it moving. Once food is in the freezer, don't just leave it there. Use it, then replace it. For quality food and economical operation, your frozen food supply should turn over about three times a year. Prepare your freezer in advance for special food sales. As you clear a space to freeze the new food, move older foods to the top or center. Check package dates and types of food, and use items within the recommended storage time.

Rearrange foods periodically, checking package information, and move older items close to the top or front, where you will use them first.

Keep a freezer notebook, to keep track of food inventory. As items are put in the freezer, record the type of food, weight or number of servings and date. As you use an item, cross it off. Before menu planning or marketing, check the notebook for foods you already have on hand.

How to Freeze

Foods which are frozen quickly form smaller ice crystals and retain better quality. Keep uncooked foods chilled until you are ready to package them. Cool hot foods in the refrigerator before packaging and placing them in the freezer.

Before adding large quantities of frozen food, clear a place for the new food. This is also a good time to check the food you already have and move it to the top or front of the freezer within easy reach.

What to Do if the Power Goes Off

If your freezer stops operating, don't open the door. Keep the chilled air inside the freezer; the food will stay frozen for a while. How long the food remains frozen depends on the weather, the location and size of your freezer, and how full it is.

The food in a full freezer at 0°F. or lower will not start to defrost for 12 to 20 hours. In a half-full freezer, defrosting will begin in a much shorter time. If operation cannot be resumed within 24 hours, you can take the food to a frozen food locker or use dry ice to keep it frozen.

Use gloves or tongs when handling dry ice to avoid burns. Place the ice on heavy cardboard laid over the food, not directly on the food packages. Avoid breathing the fumes from dry ice.

Refreezing Foods

Partial defrosting and refreezing reduces the quality and flavor of fruits, vegetables and main dishes. Meats and poultry will lose some of their juices.

If meat and poultry have defrosted completely, but are still at 40°F. or lower, they can be cooked within 24 hours and then refrozen. Check their odor and color for any signs of spoilage. If you're in doubt, don't save them. Fruit juices can be refrozen after defrosting, although quality will be impaired. Prepared foods, vegetables and especially shellfish and ice cream cannot be refrozen and should be discarded.

How to Arrange Food for Freezing

Place unfrozen food in a single layer against the walls of the freezer or quick-freeze section.

Allow 1 inch of space between packages so cold air can circulate around them.

Wait 24 hours before you stack the food and re-set the temperature control to storage position.

Freezer Storage Chart

Type		Maximum Storage Time Range
Beef		
	Roasts	8 - 9 months
	Ribs	3 - 4 months
	Steaks	6 - 8 months
	Ground	3 - 4 months
	Hamburger Patties	1 - 2 months
	Cubes	3 - 4 months
	Strips	2 - 3 months
Pork		
	Roasts	4 - 6 months
	Ribs	2 - 3 months
	Chops	3 - 4 months
	Ground	2 - 3 months
Ham	Fully Cooked	1 - 2 months
Lamb		
	Roasts	6 - 8 months
	Chops	4 - 6 months
	Cubes	3 - 4 months
	Ground	3 - 4 months
Sausage		1 - 2 months
Poultry		
	Whole Turkey	6 - 8 months
	Whole Chicken	6 - 8 months
	Cut-up Chicken	6 - 8 months
	Duckling	5 - 6 months
Other Items		
	Breads	1 - 2 months
	Cakes	1 - 3 months
	Cream Cheese	1 month
	Nuts	6 - 7 months
	Rice	1 month
	Soups	1 - 3 months

Packaging for the Microwave-Freezer Team

The quality of packaging is as important as the quality of food if you want to get as much from your freezer as you put into it. It should be moisture-proof, vapor-proof and airtight. Good packaging provides a barrier through which the natural moisture in the food cannot escape. Air, trapped inside the package, or entering through a flimsy wrap or loose seal, draws moisture from the food and produces freezer burn. The food becomes dry and tough.

Choose packaging which is suitable for the freezer. Materials designed for refrigerator storage may be inadequate for freezing. Consider your own convenience as well as the size, shape and consistency of the food. Some foods are easy to wrap or bag; others may require special attention.

Packages should be easy to store and to find when you need them. Square or rectangular packages are easier to stack than round or irregular ones. While milk, cottage cheese, sour cream or margarine cartons are not good freezer containers, they can be saved to hold airtight freezer bags.

Package Size

To make the most efficient use of the oven and freezer, and to avoid leftovers, freeze foods in meal-size or individual servings. Small packages freeze faster than large packages, forming smaller ice crystals which result in higher quality. Small amounts also defrost quickly and evenly,

with less attention. If you have a family of four, much of your food can be frozen in four-serving amounts. Freeze a few individual servings, too, for greater flexibility. They're useful when the entire family isn't home for dinner and for the person who needs to eat at a different time. If you have guests, you can defrost a family-size package, plus enough individual servings for the guests.

If your family is large, or you're cooking for a crowd, two smaller packages will freeze and defrost more efficiently than one large package.

Microwave-Freezer Packaging

In most cases, food is removed from the packaging before it is defrosted or heated. There is no need to freeze in microwave oven-proof containers. Use any freezer-proof package.

The recipes in this book direct you to freeze foods in foil-lined casseroles or freezer containers, which can be either rigid plastic or freezer bags. A few foods, like pies, are frozen in the original dish. Do not leave casseroles in the freezer once the food is frozen. They won't be available for other uses, and the defrosting and heating times are based on frozen foods in room temperature dishes. A dish which has been kept in the freezer will slow defrosting and heating because the dish will need heating also.

Quality Foods

To get high quality from the microwave-freezer team, you must put in quality. The freezer preserves the quality of foods which are sealed in airtight packages, kept at 0°F. or below, and used within the recommended storage time. The microwave brings out the flavor and texture of quality foods. Neither improve poor quality.

Buy vegetables in season, at the peak of freshness and flavor. Avoid end-of-season bargains, which may be over-mature, tough or dried out.

Buy meat and poultry from a reputable butcher, especially if you are not selecting and packaging it yourself. If you buy meat in quantity, choose a butcher who specializes in meats for home freezers, and discuss your needs with him.

How much you buy depends on your available freezer space and how much your family will consume within the recommended storage time.

Ask the butcher to remove excess fat and large bones. Have the meat cut and packaged to suit your family's taste and size. If chops and steaks are not frozen individually, ask the butcher to separate them with a double thickness of paper for easy defrosting.

Make sure he uses good quality, airtight packaging and labels the meat with cut, weight or number of servings and date. Have him quick- or flash-freeze the meat so it's freezer-ready.

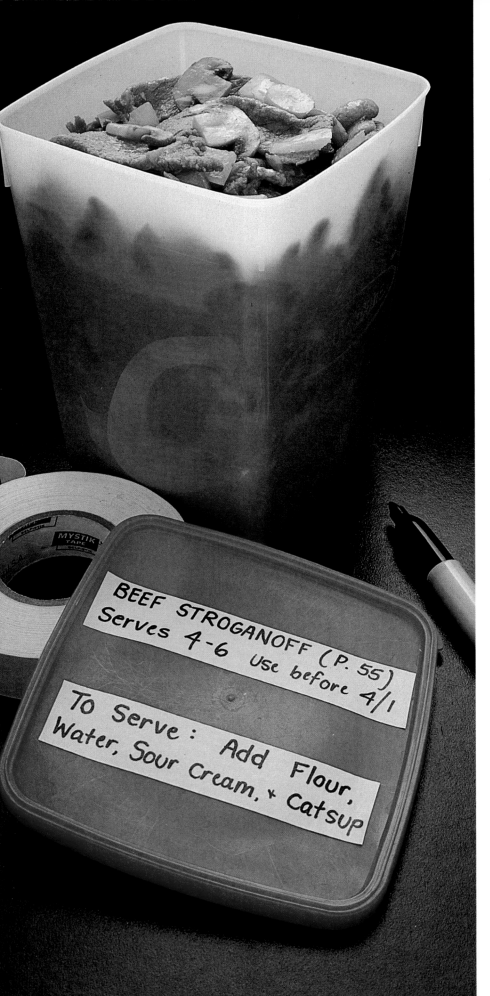

How to Label

Labeling is an important part of good freezer management. It tells you what's in the freezer and how long it's been there. Even when you're in a hurry, take the time to label clearly. Mystery packages can be frustrating and waste time later.

Use a wax crayon or waterproof marker. Write the information on a strip of freezer tape or the special labels which come with some freezer bags. You can make your own labels of sturdy paper. Attach to the package on all sides with full length strips of freezer tape. Include all the following information.

Contents. Label uncooked meats with the type, such as chicken pieces or boneless pork loin. Identify prepared foods with the recipe name and page, so you can find defrosting and heating directions easily.

Amount. List the number of servings on prepared foods or cut-up meats. Large cuts should be labeled by weight.

Date. Use the dating method which is most convenient for you. It can be the date on which the food was frozen, or the date by which it should be used or both.

Notes. Some prepared foods call for additional ingredients to complete the dish. These might be flour to thicken the sauce, grated cheese or frozen tomato sauce. Include this information on your label.

Packaging: Wraps

Wraps are excellent for large, solid, smoothly shaped items. Use them to line the inside of a dish or casserole so the food can be removed after freezing. This frees the casserole for other uses while the food is in the freezer. It also speeds defrosting and heating, because a room-temperature dish does not absorb as much heat from the food as a frozen dish.

Heavy-duty foil molds tightly against food to form an airtight package, but can develop small holes or tears in the freezer. Pad sharp or protruding edges, like bones, with crumpled foil before wrapping, or underwrap with plastic film. Heavy-duty foil is excellent for lining casseroles.

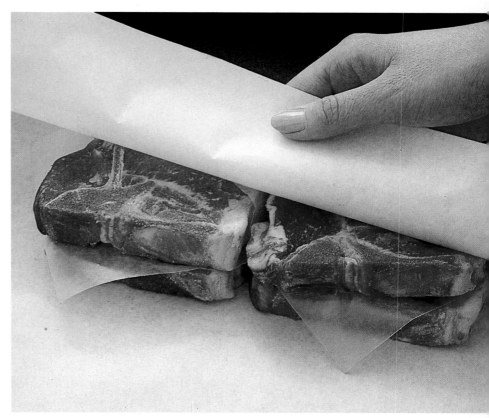

Plastic wrap makes a secure, airtight package at room temperature, but loosens in the freezer. Do not use plastic wraps by themselves in the freezer. Overwrap with foil or freezer paper.

Freezer wrap can be either wax-coated or plastic-coated. Be sure the coated, or shiny side is against the food. Press out as much air as possible. Seal all seams with freezer tape. Label by writing directly on the paper. For best results, remove wrap before defrosting. If it sticks to the food, begin defrosting and remove wrap as soon as possible.

How to Package Irregular Shapes in Foil Bundle

Place odd-shaped food on a sheet of heavy-duty foil large enough to enclose food and permit secure seal.

Pad sharp edges or underwrap. Bring corners to center in a pyramid shape, then mold foil against food.

Seal by folding excess foil over and pressing tightly against package. Label.

How to Package "Drugstore" Style

Cut freezer paper or heavy-duty foil to go around food 1½ times. Place food on foil or on coated side of freezer paper. Bring two opposite sides of wrap together; fold over 1 inch.

Continue folding, until wrap is tight against food. Press wrap tightly against food to force out air. Make package as smooth and airtight as possible.

Crease ends of wrap to form triangles. Fold up over package. Seal ends and seam of freezer paper with freezer tape. Label.

How to Package in "Casserole Wrap"

Cut piece of heavy-duty foil large enough to line casserole and leave a 1½-in. collar around edges.

Line casserole, pressing folds or wrinkles firmly against dish for a smooth surface. Add food and freeze until solid.

Lift food from casserole with foil. Cover with heavy-duty foil the size of dish, plus collar. Press out air. Fold edges up and over; press together. Label.

How to Package "Butcher" Style

Cut freezer wrap or heavy-duty foil 3 times as large as food. Place food on foil or on coated side of freezer paper diagonally near one corner with wrap extending beyond ends of food.

Fold short corner over food, then fold sides of wrap up over food tightly, pressing out air.

Roll up to opposite corner of wrap, continuously folding sides tight against food. Keep package smooth and airtight. Seal free corner with freezer tape. Label.

Packaging: Bags

Versatile, freezer-weight bags come in a variety of sizes and can be used for the same products as either wraps or rigid containers. Be sure to use freezer-weight bags; refrigerator storage bags are not sufficiently vapor- and moisture-proof for freezer storage.

There are two types of freezer bags. Reclosable bags are especially useful for loose-packing. Heat-sealable bags or pouches, like those used for convenience vegetables and entrees, are available for home freezing and can be used in the microwave oven. If you use a heat sealer, be sure you use heat-sealable bags, as the manufacturer directs.

Solid items, like roasts or poultry can be packed in bags. They will be similar in size and shape to wrapped items. Bags of sauced foods, like cooked main dishes, can be difficult to store. You can save milk cartons to give shape to foods stored in bags.

Sauced foods, such as chili, soups and stews expand during freezing, and will require head space in bags as they do in rigid containers. How much head space is needed depends on the amount and type of food. Allow about ½ to 1 inch for a pint of food, 1 to 2 inches for a quart, and more if the food is very liquid.

Freeze bags flat to simplify storage. They will be easier to stack and organize.

How to Bag Solid Foods

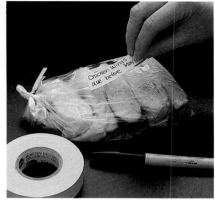

Choose a bag large enough to enclose the food and allow for sealing space at the top.

Press bag against the food to expel air through the opening. Seal bag as directed below.

Label bags with a strip of freezer tape.

How to Bag Sauced Foods

Support bag in a carton, freezer box, measure or bowl. Add food, allowing head space and room for sealing.

Close bag opening above food, squeezing out air.

Seal above head space, as directed below. Pull out any deep folds which would be trapped in food as it freezes.

How to Seal Freezer Bags & Heat-Sealable Bags

Use goose-neck seal on reclosable bags. Twist top of bag for about 2 inches. Fold bag over against twist; secure with twist tie.

Heat-seal pouches following manufacturer's directions.

Packaging: Containers

Freezing in containers offers several advantages. Containers stack easily in the freezer, allowing better organization. Some products are packaged in containers which can be saved.

Rigid plastic freezer containers are available in a variety of sizes. They are popular because they are easy to stack, have tight fitting lids and are durable.

Sturdy plastic containers can be saved from many foods like ice cream, sherbet and some margarines. Do not use containers that do not have tight fitting lids. Lightweight, brittle cartons, such as those containing cottage cheese or deli-foods are not sturdy enough for freezer use.

Waxed freezer cartons can be purchased for use with freezer bags. They store flat until ready to use and can be reused. Always use with freezer bags; the waxed freezer cartons are not airtight.

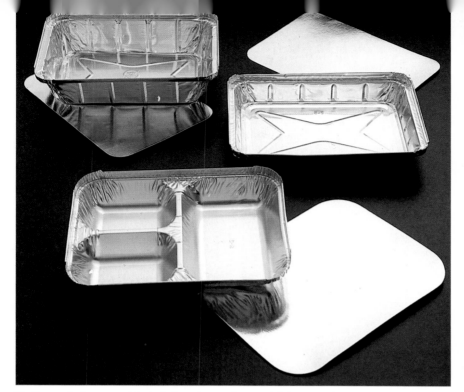

Foil containers with foil-lined cardboard lids can be purchased in hardware stores and supermarkets. Save frozen entrée containers; use foil for a cover.

Waxed paper cartons from milk and sour cream can be washed and used with freezer bags. The cartons shape the food, making it easier to stack.

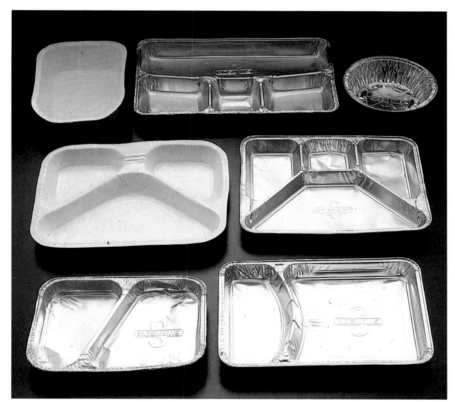

Ovenable paper and foil TV dinner trays can be purchased or saved from convenience foods, but the lids are not reusable. The trays do not seal airtight, so should be stored in the freezer no longer than 1 month.

Label containers with freezer tape or make paper labels and tape them securely on all sides of containers.

Packaging: Containers (continued)

How to Package in Rigid Plastic Containers

Allow head space of ½ inch for a pint or 1 inch for a quart when filling containers with sauced foods which expand.

Fill in extra air space in containers by freezing the food until solid, then covering with crumpled foil, plastic or freezer wrap before sealing.

Seal airtight. Overwrap containers that do not have airtight lids with foil, freezer paper or freezer bag. Label.

How to Package in Foil Containers

Place food in container, allowing head space for sauced foods to expand.

Place foil-lined lid on tray. Crimp edge of tray tightly over lid to seal. Label.

Seal tray with heavy-duty foil if lid is not available. Crimp tightly over edges of tray. Label.

How to Package in Waxed Cartons

Line carton with freezer bag. Carefully spoon cooled food into freezer bag.

Gather top of bag together, pressing out air and allowing head space for sauced foods.

Seal above head space with goose neck twist, as directed on page 17. Label.

How to Package in TV Dinner Trays

Place main course in large compartment of foil or ovenable paper TV dinner tray.

Spoon remaining food evenly into small section. Surface of food should not be higher than rim of tray.

Seal tray with heavy-duty foil. Crimp foil tightly over edges of tray. For extra protection, seal covered tray in freezer bag.

21

TV Dinners

Package your own TV dinners in foil or ovenable paper trays. These dinners are made with foods from this book which heat together evenly in the same amount of time. To make your own combinations, you will need to experiment with the times and check food often.

Scallop-Salmon Kabobs With Vegetable-Rice Mix & Peas

Scallop-Salmon Kabobs,
  page 106
Vegetable-Rice Mix,
  page 126
4 cups frozen peas
⅓ cup butter or margarine
8 TV dinner trays, 3
  compartments each

Makes 8 TV dinners

Prepare Scallop-Salmon Kabobs as directed. Place one kabob in main compartment of each tray. Prepare Vegetable-Rice Mix as directed. Divide in half. Label and freeze one half. Divide other half and spoon into small compartment of each tray.

Place ½ cup peas in each remaining tray compartment. Place butter in small bowl. Microwave at High 45 to 60 seconds, or until melted. Spoon equally over peas in each tray. Wrap each tray individually. Label and freeze no longer than 1 month.

To serve, unwrap one tray and place in microwave oven. Cover with wax paper. Microwave at 50% (Medium) 10 to 13 minutes, or until scallops are opaque and flake easily, turning kabob over after half the time and rotating tray once.

Stuffed Shrimp With Wild Rice & Broccoli

Stuffed Shrimp, page 110
Wild Rice, page 126
2 cups frozen chopped
  broccoli
2 tablespoons plus 2 tea-
  spoons butter or margarine

½ teaspoon lemon pepper
4 TV dinner trays, 3
  compartments each

Makes 4 TV dinners

Prepare Stuffed Shrimp as directed. Divide equally among main tray compartments. Prepare Wild Rice as directed. Divide in half. Label and freeze. Divide other half and spoon into small compartment of each tray.

Place ½ cup broccoli in each remaining tray compartment. In small bowl combine butter and lemon pepper. Microwave at High 30 to 45 seconds, or until butter melts. Spoon equally over broccoli in each tray. Wrap each tray individually. Label and freeze no longer than 1 month.

To serve, unwrap one tray and place in microwave oven. Cover with wax paper. Microwave at 70% (Medium-High) 4 to 7 minutes, or until shrimp are opaque, rearranging shrimp and rotating tray after half the time.

Rolled Beef Swirls With Gnocchi & Green Beans

Rolled Beef Swirls, page 64
Gnocchi in Tomato Sauce,
    page 125
8 TV dinner trays, 3
    compartments each
4 cups frozen green beans
¼ cup plus 1 tablespoon butter
    or margarine

To serve:
1 slice bacon

Makes 8 TV dinners

How to Microwave Rolled Beef Swirls Dinner

Prepare Rolled Beef Swirls and Gnocchi in Tomato Sauce as directed. Divide equally among eight trays.

Place ½ cup beans in remaining compartment of each tray. Melt butter in custard cup at High 45 seconds to 1¼ minutes.

Spoon equally over beans in each tray. Wrap each tray individually. Label and freeze no longer than 1 month.

To serve, place bacon on paper towel. Microwave at High 45 to 60 seconds, or until brown. Crumble.

Unwrap one tray. Sprinkle bacon over green beans. Cover with wax paper. Place in microwave oven.

Microwave TV dinner at 70% (Medium-High) 6 to 9 minutes, or until meat is cooked to desired doneness, turning meat over and rotating tray once.

Tangy Short Ribs & Twice Baked Potato

Tangy Short Ribs, page 57
Twice Baked Potatoes,
   page 122
4 TV dinner trays, 2
   compartments each

To serve:
1 tablespoon shredded
   Cheddar cheese

      Makes 4 TV dinners

Prepare Tangy Short Ribs as directed. Divide ribs equally among trays. Divide and pour equal amounts of tangy sauce over ribs.

Prepare Twice Baked Potatoes. Place one potato in each tray. Freeze remaining potatoes.

Freeze until firm. Wrap, label and freeze no longer than 1 month.

To serve, unwrap one tray and place in microwave oven. Cover with wax paper. Microwave at 70% (Medium-High) 9 to 12 minutes, or until heated, rotating tray 1 or 2 times and turning ribs over once. Sprinkle cheese on potato during last minute of cooking. Let stand, covered, 5 minutes before serving. Serve with salad, if desired.

Chicken With Rice Stuffing, Carrots & Brussels Sprouts ▶

Rice-Stuffed Chicken
Breasts, page 97
4 TV dinner trays, 3
compartments each
2 cups frozen carrots
½ cup orange juice
¼ cup plus 3 tablespoons
butter or margarine, divided
2 cups frozen Brussels
sprouts

Makes 4 TV dinners

Prepare Rice-Stuffed Chicken Breasts as directed. Place one rolled breast in main compartment of each tray. Place ½ cup carrots in small compartment of each tray.

Combine orange juice and ¼ cup butter in 2-cup measure. Microwave at High 2 to 3 minutes, or until butter melts. Pour equally over carrots in each tray.

Place ½ cup Brussels sprouts in each remaining tray compartment. Place remaining 3 tablespoons butter in custard cup. Microwave at High 30 to 45 seconds, or until melted. Pour equally over Brussels sprouts in each tray. Wrap each tray individually. Label and freeze no longer than 1 month.

To serve, unwrap one tray and place in microwave oven. Cover with wax paper. Microwave at 50% (Medium) 8 to 15 minutes, or until chicken is no longer pink and vegetables are heated, turning chicken breast over after half the time, and rotating tray 1 or 2 times.

Tomato-Mushroom Chicken & Vegetable Rice Mix

Tomato-Mushroom Chicken,
page 98
Vegetable-Rice Mix, page 126

6 TV dinner trays, 2
compartments each

Makes 6 TV dinners

Prepare Tomato-Mushroom Chicken as directed. Divide equally among trays.

Prepare Vegetable-Rice Mix as directed. Freeze one half of recipe. Divide remaining half equally among trays. Freeze until firm. Wrap, label and freeze no longer than 1 month.

To serve, unwrap one tray and place in microwave oven. Cover with wax paper. Microwave at High 6 to 10 minutes, or until heated, rotating tray and stirring rice and chicken once. Serve with salad, if desired.

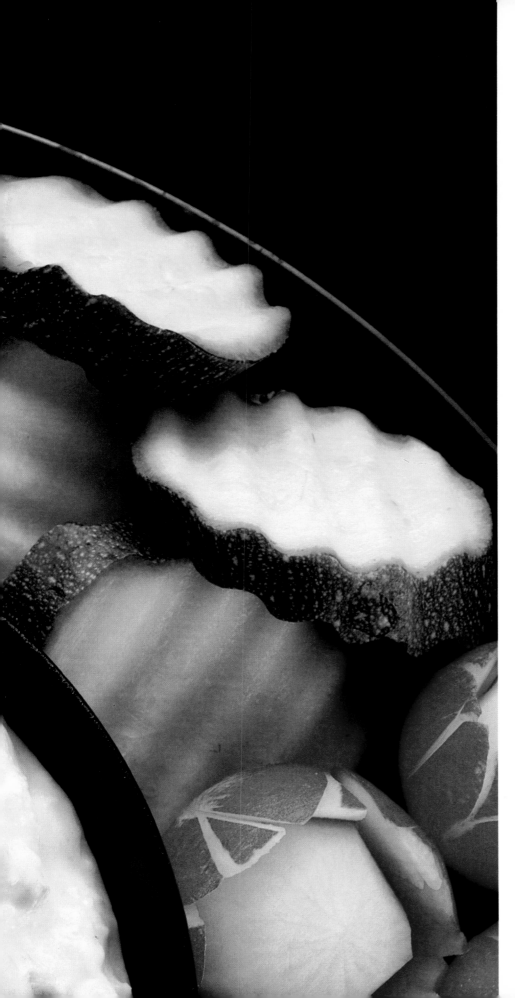

Appetizers

Entertain with ease. Whether your party is planned in advance or impromptu, you can treat your guests to appetizers. Prepare and freeze them ahead of time, then microwave at serving time.

Shrimp Dip

3 tablespoons chopped green onion
2 tablespoons chopped celery
1 tablespoon butter or margarine
2 cans (4¼ oz. each) tiny shrimp, drained and chopped
2 hard cooked eggs, finely chopped, optional
1 teaspoon prepared mustard
Dash cayenne
1½ cups small-curd cottage cheese
½ cup milk

Makes 2 dips
1½ cups each

Place green onion, celery and butter in 1-qt. casserole. Microwave at High 45 seconds to 1½ minutes, or until celery is tender-crisp. Stir in shrimp, eggs, mustard and cayenne. Set aside.

In blender or food processor blend cottage cheese and milk until smooth. Stir into shrimp mixture. Spoon into two freezer containers. Label and freeze no longer than 1 month.

To serve, remove from one container and place in 1-qt. casserole. Microwave at 50% (Medium) 5 to 8 minutes, or until defrosted but still cold, breaking apart and stirring with a fork several times. Garnish with additional chopped green onion, if desired. Serve with vegetable dippers or crackers, if desired.

29

Guacamole ▲

4 slices bacon
2 medium ripe avocados
1 tablespoon lemon juice
½ teaspoon onion salt
¼ teaspoon chili powder

To serve:
1 small tomato, chopped

Makes 1¾ cups

Arrange bacon on three layers of paper towel. Cover with paper towel. Microwave at High 3 to 4 minutes, or until crisp. Let stand 3 to 5 minutes.

Peel and pit avocados. In medium bowl mash avocados with lemon juice, onion salt and chili powder. Crumble bacon. Stir into avocado mixture. Spoon into freezer container. Label and freeze no longer than 1 month.

To serve, remove from container and place in 1-qt. casserole or serving bowl. Microwave at 50% (Medium) 4 to 5 minutes, or until defrosted but still cold, breaking up once. Let stand 5 minutes. Stir in tomato. Serve with corn chips, if desired.

Chili Con Queso ▲

1 can (28 oz.) whole tomatoes
2 cans (4 oz. each) green chilies, drained and chopped
2 medium green peppers, chopped
1 cup chopped fresh mushrooms, optional
1 large onion, chopped
1 large clove garlic, minced
2 teaspoons chili powder

To serve:
3 cups shredded Monterey Jack cheese
1 tablespoon all-purpose flour
½ cup chilled whipping cream

Makes 2 dips
3½ to 4 cups each

In 3-qt. casserole combine tomatoes, green chilies, green peppers, mushrooms, onion, garlic and chili powder. Break up tomatoes with spoon. Microwave at High 1¼ to 1½ hours, or until moisture is gone, stirring 2 or 3 times. Spoon into two freezer containers. Label and freeze no longer than 6 months.

To serve, shake cheese and flour in bag to coat cheese. Remove tomato mixture from one container and place in deep bowl. Microwave at High 6 to 8 minutes, or until very hot, stirring 1 or 2 times to break up frozen portions. Stir in cheese and cream. Reduce power to 50% (Medium). Microwave 3 to 5 minutes, or until cheese melts, blending 2 or 3 times. Serve with taco chips, if desired.

Cocktail Ribs

Ribs:
4½ to 5 lbs. pork spareribs, cut in half across bones,* then into single rib pieces
1 large onion, cut into eighths
1 small lemon, thinly sliced
2 stalks celery, cut into 1-in. pieces
1 teaspoon salt
¼ teaspoon dried marjoram leaves
5 or 6 whole peppercorns
½ cup hot water

Sauce:
1½ cups catsup
⅓ cup chili sauce
⅓ cup honey
3 tablespoons soy sauce
⅛ teaspoon garlic powder

Makes about 2 dozen

Place ribs in 5-qt. casserole. Top with onion, lemon, celery, salt, marjoram and peppercorns. Pour in water; cover. Microwave at High 5 minutes. Reduce power to 50% (Medium). Microwave 1¼ to 1¾ hours, or until fork tender, stirring to rearrange 2 or 3 times. Let stand, covered, 10 minutes. Drain and discard liquid.

Combine all sauce ingredients in small bowl. Package one-third of ribs and one-third of sauce in each of three freezer containers. Label and freeze no longer than 3 months.

To serve, remove from one container and place in 8 × 8-in. baking dish. Cover with plastic wrap. Microwave at 70% (Medium-High) 5 minutes, breaking apart with fork. Microwave, covered, at 70% (Medium-High) 3 to 6 minutes, or until heated, stirring 1 or 2 times. Repeat, as desired.

*Ask your butcher to do this when meat is purchased.

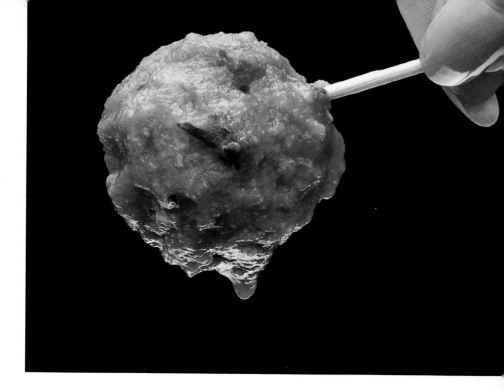

Mexican Meatballs ▲

Meatballs:
¼ cup finely chopped onion
1 clove garlic, minced
1 tablespoon olive oil
1 lb. ground beef
⅓ cup dry bread crumbs
1 teaspoon dry mustard
½ teaspoon salt
¼ teaspoon pepper
1 egg
2 tablespoons chopped green chilies

Sauce:
3 cans (8 oz. each) tomato sauce or 3 containers Tomato Sauce, defrosted, page 123
1 tablespoon snipped fresh parsley
¾ teaspoon chili powder
½ teaspoon sugar
¼ teaspoon ground cumin

Makes 3 dozen

Place onion, garlic and olive oil in medium bowl or 2-qt. casserole. Microwave at High 2 minutes, or until onion is tender. Mix in remaining meatball ingredients.

Shape by tablespoonfuls into 36 meatballs, about 1¼ inches in diameter. Place in 12 × 8-in. baking dish. Cover with wax paper. Microwave at High 4 to 5½ minutes, or until set but still slightly pink, rearranging and turning over after half the time. Drain; arrange meatballs on wax paper-lined tray large enough so meatballs do not touch. Freeze until firm.

Combine sauce ingredients in small bowl. Microwave at High 1 to 2½ minutes, or until heated. Package one-third of meatballs and one-third of sauce in each of three freezer containers. Label and freeze no longer than 1 month.

To serve, remove from one container and place in 1-qt. casserole or bowl. Cover with wax paper. Microwave at 70% (Medium-High) 8 to 14 minutes, or until meatballs are defrosted and sauce is hot, breaking apart with fork after 5 minutes and stirring 1 or 2 times. Repeat, as desired.

Chicken-Pineapple Canapés

- 1½ lbs. boneless chicken breasts
- ⅓ cup finely chopped celery
- ⅓ cup finely chopped green pepper
- 3 tablespoons finely chopped onion
- 1 tablespoon butter or margarine
- 1 pkg. (8 oz.) cream cheese
- 1 can (8¼ oz.) crushed pineapple, drained
- ⅓ cup chopped cashews
- 1 tablespoon snipped fresh parsley
- 1½ teaspoons lemon juice
- ¼ teaspoon salt
  Dash pepper
- 15 slices wheat and white bread

Makes about 5 dozen

Place chicken breasts in 1½-qt. casserole; cover. Microwave at High 8 to 10 minutes, or until chicken is no longer pink. Cool. Discard skin and cooking liquid. Chop into small pieces.

In medium bowl combine celery, green pepper, onion and butter. Microwave at High 2 to 4 minutes, or until vegetables are tender-crisp. Add cream cheese. Microwave at High 20 to 30 seconds, or until cream cheese softens. Stir in chicken, pineapple, cashews, parsley, lemon juice, salt and pepper.

Trim crusts from bread. Spread filling on bread. With knife or small cookie cutter, cut each slice of bread into four shapes. Sprinkle with paprika, if desired. Freeze on tray until firm. Wrap, label and freeze no longer than 3 weeks.

To serve, unwrap 12; arrange in circle on large plate. Microwave at 50% (Medium) 4½ to 6½ minutes, or until defrosted but still cold, rotating and rearranging canapés once. Let stand 5 minutes. Repeat, as desired.

Ham & Swiss Canapés ▲

- 1 container (8 oz.) Swiss almond cheese food
- 1 can (4½ oz.) deviled ham
- 1½ teaspoons chopped chives
  Dash cayenne

- 36 to 48 almond slices, optional

To serve:
36 to 48 crackers

Makes 3 to 4 dozen

Place cheese food in small bowl or 1-qt. casserole. Microwave at High 30 to 45 seconds, or until softened. Mix in deviled ham, chives and cayenne.

Using pastry bag and number 6 star tip, pipe canapé mixture onto wax paper-lined tray, making rosettes about 1¼ inches in diameter. (If mixture is too soft, refrigerate until it reaches the correct consistency.) Top each rosette with almond slice. Freeze until firm. Package in freezer containers. Label and freeze no longer than 1 month.

To serve, remove 12 rosettes from container and center on 12 crackers. Arrange in circle on paper towel-lined plate. Microwave at 30% (Medium-Low) 45 seconds to 2 minutes, or until rosettes are softened, rotating plate every 30 seconds. Let stand 1 to 2 minutes. Repeat, as desired.

Spinach-Ham Canapés

2 pkgs. (10 oz. each) frozen
    chopped spinach
½ cup finely chopped onion
1 large clove garlic, minced
1 tablespoon olive oil
2 tablespoons all-purpose flour
24 nut cups, 1¾ × 1¼-in.
1 pkg. (8 oz.) cream cheese
2 eggs
1 can (6½ oz.) chunk ham
⅛ teaspoon pepper
¾ cup shredded Cheddar
    cheese

          Makes 2 dozen

How to Microwave Spinach-Ham Canapés

Place spinach packages in oven. Microwave at High 4 to 6 minutes, or until warm. Drain spinach, pressing out excess moisture. Set aside.

Combine onion, garlic and olive oil in medium bowl. Microwave at High 1 to 2 minutes, or until onion is tender. Mix in spinach and flour.

Press a scant tablespoonful of spinach mixture over bottom and sides of nut cups to form a shell. Set aside.

Place cream cheese in medium bowl. Microwave at 50% (Medium) 45 to 60 seconds, or until softened. Blend remaining ingredients into cream cheese.

Spoon mixture into spinach-lined cups. Freeze on tray until firm. Wrap, label and freeze no longer than 1 month.

To serve, unwrap 12; remove cups. Arrange on plate. Cover with wax paper. Microwave at 50% (Medium) 8 to 12 minutes, or until centers are just set, rearranging 3 times. Let stand 5 to 10 minutes. Repeat, as desired.

◄ Miniature Cheese Balls

1 pkg. (8 oz.) cream cheese
½ cup shredded Cheddar
   cheese
1 container (8 oz.) sharp
   Cheddar cheese food
¼ cup finely chopped green
   onion
1 clove garlic, minced
1 tablespoon butter or
   margarine
1 tablespoon Worcestershire
   sauce
1 tablespoon brandy
1 tablespoon snipped fresh
   parsley
1 teaspoon paprika
6 drops red pepper sauce
1½ cups finely chopped
   pecans

Makes 4 dozen

Place cream cheese and shredded Cheddar cheese in 2-qt. casserole. Microwave at High 30 seconds. Add Cheddar cheese food. Microwave at High 20 to 30 seconds, or until cheeses soften. Beat until smooth.

Place onion, garlic and butter in small bowl. Microwave at High 30 to 45 seconds, or until onion is tender. Mix into cheese mixture with Worcestershire sauce, brandy, parsley, paprika and red pepper sauce.

Refrigerate at least 2 hours. Shape by tablespoonfuls into 48 balls. Roll in pecans. Arrange on wax paper-lined tray large enough so cheese balls do not touch. Freeze until firm. Package in freezer containers. Label and freeze no longer than 1 month.

To serve, remove 12 cheese balls from container and place in circle on serving plate. Microwave at 30% (Medium-Low) 45 seconds to 2 minutes, or until defrosted but still cool, rotating plate ½ turn every 30 seconds. Let stand 3 to 5 minutes before serving. Repeat, as desired.

Wheat-Cheese Thins ▲

1½ cups shredded Cheddar
   cheese
¾ cup all-purpose flour
¾ cup whole wheat flour
¾ cup butter or margarine
¾ teaspoon caraway seed,
   optional

4 to 6 drops red pepper
   sauce
Grated Parmesan cheese
Paprika

Makes about 6 dozen

In medium bowl combine Cheddar cheese, flours, butter, caraway seed and red pepper sauce. Beat with electric mixer until blended. Roll out to ⅛-in. thickness on wheat-floured surface. Cut with small cookie cutters. Sprinkle with Parmesan cheese and paprika. Freeze on trays until firm. Package in three freezer containers with wax paper between layers. Label and freeze no longer than 2 weeks.

To serve, remove from one container and place on baking sheet. Microwave at High 3 to 6½ minutes, or until cheese thins appear dry, rotating 2 or 3 times. Let stand 1 minute. Remove to wire rack to cool. Repeat, as desired.

Blue Cheese Log

2 teaspoons butter or
  margarine
3 tablespoons sesame seed
2 pkgs. (8 oz. each) cream
  cheese
1 pkg. (4 oz.) blue cheese
1 cup shredded Cheddar
  cheese
1 tablespoon sherry
1 tablespoon Worcestershire
  sauce
¼ teaspoon onion powder
⅛ teaspoon garlic powder

Makes two 6-in. logs

Melt butter in pie plate at High
30 to 45 seconds. Stir in
sesame seed to coat. Microwave at High 5 to 10 minutes,
or until light brown, stirring
every other minute. Set aside.

In 2-qt. casserole place cream
cheese, blue cheese and
Cheddar cheese. Reduce
power to 50% (Medium).
Microwave 1 to 2½ minutes, or
until cheeses soften. Add
sherry, Worcestershire sauce,
onion powder and garlic
powder. Beat with electric mixer
until fluffy. Refrigerate 1 to 2
hours, or until mixture can be
handled easily.

Divide chilled mixture in half.
Using wax paper, shape each
half into a 6-in. log. Roll each
log in toasted sesame seed.
Wrap separately, label and
freeze no longer than 1 month.

To serve, unwrap one log and
place on plate. Microwave at
30% (Medium-Low) 2 to 4
minutes, or until wooden pick
can be easily inserted in center,
rotating plate every minute. Let
stand 10 to 15 minutes. Serve
with crackers, if desired.

Parmesan-Bacon Spread ▶

12 slices bacon
1 cup unsalted butter
1 pkg. (8 oz.) cream cheese
⅔ cup grated Parmesan
  cheese
3 tablespoons chopped green
  onion
8 to 10 drops red pepper
  sauce

Makes 2 spreads
1¼ cups each

Place bacon in 2- to 3-qt.
casserole. Microwave at High 8
to 12 minutes, or until crisp.
Drain on paper towels.
Crumble; set aside.

In medium bowl combine butter
and cream cheese. Microwave
at 50% (Medium) 30 to 60
seconds, or until butter softens.
Mix in crumbled bacon and
remaining ingredients.

Line two small bowls with foil,
flattening wrinkles. If desired,
lightly butter foil and coat with
additional Parmesan cheese
and paprika. Spoon cheese-
bacon mixture into foil. Press
into shape of bowls. Freeze until
firm. Remove with foil from bowls.
Wrap separately, label and
freeze no longer than 1 month.

To serve, unwrap one package
and place on plate. Microwave
at 30% (Medium-Low) 1½ to 3
minutes, or until slightly defrosted,
taking care not to melt edge,
and rotating 2 or 3 times. Let
stand 10 to 15 minutes. Serve
with crackers, if desired.

Soups

Soups are excellent dishes for the microwave oven and freezer. They store well in the freezer and defrost and heat quickly in the microwave oven. Most of these soups are substantial enough to serve as a supper with a salad and a crusty bread.

Bouillabaisse

1 medium onion, cut in half and thinly sliced
2 stalks celery, chopped
2 tablespoons olive oil
3 cups hot water
1 can (15 oz.) tomato sauce
1 cup white wine
3 tomatoes, peeled, cut in half and sliced
1 small orange, thinly sliced
3 slices lemon
1 small clove garlic, minced
3 tablespoons butter or margarine
2 teaspoons sugar

¼ teaspoon dried bouquet garni seasoning
¼ teaspoon cayenne
⅛ teaspoon ground saffron
1 lb. red snapper or halibut fillet, cut into 2- to 3-in. pieces
10 to 12-oz. fresh lobster tail, cut in half crosswise, shell left on
½ lb. fresh medium shrimp, peeled and deveined, tails left on
½ lb. fresh scallops

Makes 2 soups
4 to 6 servings each

In 5-qt. casserole combine onion, celery and olive oil; cover. Microwave at High 6 to 9 minutes, or until vegetables are tender, stirring every 3 minutes. Stir in remaining ingredients except fish and seafood; cover. Microwave at High 25 to 30 minutes, or until flavors blend and tomatoes are tender, stirring 2 or 3 times.

Stir in fish and seafood. Reduce power to 50% (Medium). Microwave 3 to 5 minutes, or until fish flakes easily and seafood is opaque, stirring once. Spoon into two freezer containers. Label and freeze no longer than 1 month.

To serve, remove from one container and place in 2-qt. casserole. Microwave at 50% (Medium) 40 to 55 minutes, or until heated, breaking apart and stirring every 5 minutes.

◄ Tomato-Vegetable Soup

6 medium tomatoes, peeled and chopped
2 cups water
1 can (10½ oz.) condensed tomato soup
1 tablespoon plus 1 teaspoon instant chicken bouillon granules
1 tablespoon sugar
½ teaspoon dried basil leaves
¼ teaspoon dried savory leaves
¼ teaspoon pepper
⅛ teaspoon ground sage
½ lb. broccoli
2 cups cauliflowerets, cut into 1-in. pieces
1 medium onion, cut into ½-in. wedges
⅓ cup uncooked instant rice

Makes 2 soups
4 to 6 servings each

In 3-qt. casserole combine tomatoes, water, tomato soup, bouillon granules, sugar, basil, savory, pepper and sage; cover. Microwave at High 40 minutes, stirring 2 or 3 times to break apart tomatoes. Cut broccoli into flowerets. Remove and discard lower stalk; cut upper stalk into thin slices. Stir in broccoli, cauliflowerets, and onion; cover. Microwave at High 15 to 30 minutes, or until vegetables are tender, stirring 1 or 2 times. Stir in rice. Spoon into two freezer containers. Label and freeze no longer than 2 months.

To serve, remove from one container and place in 1½-qt. casserole; cover. Microwave at High 17 to 25 minutes, or until heated, breaking apart and stirring every 10 minutes.

NOTE: To peel tomatoes, place 3 quarts hot water in 5-qt. casserole; cover. Microwave at High 18 to 25 minutes, or until boiling. Place tomatoes in water. Let stand 30 seconds to 1½ minutes, or until skins begin to loosen. Plunge tomatoes into cold water. Remove skins.

Clam Chowder

½ cup hot water
1 pint clams in shells
4 slices bacon, cut up
1 cup cubed peeled red potatoes, ¼-in. cubes
1 small onion, chopped
2 tablespoons all-purpose flour
1 cup milk
½ teaspoon salt
⅛ teaspoon white pepper
Dash celery salt
½ cup half and half

Serves 4 to 6

Pour water into 2-qt. casserole; cover. Microwave at High 1 to 2 minutes, or until boiling. Add clams. Microwave at High 1½ to 3 minutes, or until shells open. Remove clams; clean and mince. Discard cooking liquid.

Place bacon in 2-qt. casserole. Microwave at High 3 to 5 minutes, or until crisp, stirring once. Remove bacon. Set aside. Drain all but 2 tablespoons bacon drippings. Add potatoes and onion; cover. Microwave at High 2½ to 5½ minutes, or until potatoes are tender-crisp. Mix in flour. Stir in milk, salt, white pepper and celery salt. Microwave, uncovered, at High 2½ to 4½ minutes, or until thickened, stirring 2 or 3 times. Add clams, bacon and half and half. Spoon into freezer container. Label and freeze no longer than 1 month.

To serve, remove from container and place in 1-qt. casserole; cover. Microwave at 50% (Medium) 17 to 23 minutes, or until heated, breaking apart and stirring 3 or 4 times.

Spanish Hot Pot

¼ lb. salt pork, cut into ½-in. cubes
1 medium onion, chopped
1 medium green pepper, chopped
1 clove garlic, minced
3 cups cubed peeled red potatoes, ½-in. cubes
2½ cups hot water
1 can (16 oz.) Great Northern beans, drained and rinsed
1¼ teaspoons sugar
1 teaspoon instant chicken bouillon granules
1 teaspoon instant beef bouillon granules
¼ teaspoon ground nutmeg
¼ teaspoon pepper
1 pkg. (10 oz.) frozen turnip greens

Makes 2 soups
4 to 6 servings each

In 3-qt. casserole place salt pork, onion, green pepper and garlic; cover. Microwave at High 4 to 8 minutes, or until vegetables are tender, stirring 2 or 3 times. Stir in potatoes, water, beans, sugar, chicken and beef bouillon granules, nutmeg and pepper. Add turnip greens; cover.

Microwave at High 10 minutes, stirring with fork to break apart greens. Reduce power to 70% (Medium-High). Microwave 15 to 26 minutes, or until potatoes and greens are tender, stirring 2 or 3 times. Spoon into two freezer containers. Label and freeze no longer than 3 months.

To serve, remove from one container and place in 1½-qt. casserole; cover. Microwave at High 12 to 15 minutes, or until heated, breaking apart and stirring 2 or 3 times.

Vichyssoise ►

4 medium potatoes, peeled and thinly sliced
2 teaspoons instant chicken bouillon granules
½ cup hot water
¼ cup butter or margarine, divided
2 cups half and half, divided
½ cup finely chopped onion
¼ teaspoon salt
⅛ teaspoon white pepper

Serves 4 to 6

Place potatoes in 2-qt. casserole. Stir bouillon into hot water. Pour over potatoes; cover. Microwave at High 9 to 12 minutes, or until tender, stirring 1 or 2 times. Remove potatoes with liquid to large bowl. Add 3 tablespoons of the butter and ½ cup of the half and half. Mash potatoes until smooth, using electric mixer.

In 2-qt. casserole combine onion and remaining 1 tablespoon butter; cover. Microwave at High 2 to 3½ minutes, or until tender, stirring once. Mix onion, remaining 1½ cups half and half, the salt and pepper into potatoes. Spoon into freezer container. Label and freeze no longer than 2 months.

To serve cold, remove from container and place in 1½-qt. casserole; cover. Microwave at 70% (Medium-High) 7 to 10 minutes, breaking apart 2 or 3 times. (Some icy pieces will remain.) Let stand 5 to 10 minutes to complete defrosting. Garnish with snipped fresh chives, if desired.

To serve hot, prepare as directed above, except omit standing time. Continue microwaving at 70% (Medium-High) 6 to 9 minutes, or until heated, breaking apart and stirring 2 or 3 times. Garnish with snipped fresh chives, if desired.

Cabbage Soup

1 ham bone
6 cups hot water
1 cup diagonally sliced carrot,
  ½-in. slices
¾ cup diagonally sliced celery,
  ½-in. slices
¼ cup chopped onion
1 clove garlic, minced
1 bay leaf
½ teaspoon dried basil leaves
¼ teaspoon pepper
8 cups coarsely chopped
  cabbage
½ lb. chorizo sausage, cut into
  1-in. slices

Makes 2 soups
4 to 6 servings each

In 5-qt. casserole combine ham
bone, water, carrot, celery,
onion, garlic, bay leaf, basil and
pepper; cover. Microwave at
High 45 minutes, turning ham
bone over after every 15 minutes.
Remove ham bone. Stir in
cabbage and sausage; cover.

Microwave at High 5 to 12
minutes, or until cabbage is
tender-crisp, stirring 2 or 3
times. Cut ham from bone; trim
fat. Discard fat and bone. Cut
ham into small pieces and
return to soup. Spoon into two
freezer containers. Label and
freeze no longer than 2 months.

To serve, remove from one
container and place in 2-qt.
casserole; cover. Microwave at
70% (Medium-High) 17 to 25
minutes, or until heated,
breaking apart and stirring 2 or
3 times.

Pumpkin Soup

8 lb. pumpkin, cut in half,
  seeds and pulp removed
⅓ cup finely chopped onion
¼ cup butter or margarine
3 cups hot water
2 tablespoons instant chicken
  bouillon granules
¼ teaspoon ground nutmeg
⅛ teaspoon white pepper
⅛ teaspoon ground ginger
⅛ teaspoon ground allspice
1 stick cinnamon
½ cup half and half

Makes 2 soups
4 to 6 servings each

Place one-half of pumpkin in
8 × 8-in. baking dish. Cover with
plastic wrap. Microwave at High
10 to 15 minutes, or until tender,
rotating dish every 5 minutes.
Repeat with remaining half.
Spoon pumpkin from shell.
Mash or process in food processor until smooth. Set aside.

Place onion and butter in 5-qt.
casserole; cover. Microwave at
High 3 to 5½ minutes, or until
tender, stirring once. Mix in
mashed pumpkin and remaining
ingredients. Reduce power to
50% (Medium). Microwave,
uncovered, 8 to 10 minutes, or
until flavors blend, stirring 2 or 3
times. Spoon into two freezer
containers. Label and freeze no
longer than 2 months.

To serve, remove from one
container and place in 1½-qt.
casserole. Microwave at 50%
(Medium) 17 to 21 minutes, or
until heated, breaking apart and
stirring 2 or 3 times.

Garlic Soup

10 medium cloves garlic
1 small onion, thinly sliced
1 tablespoon olive oil
3 cups hot water
1 can (10½ oz.) condensed
  beef broth
¼ teaspoon dry mustard
⅛ teaspoon dried thyme leaves
  Dash dried marjoram leaves
½ cup shredded carrot

To serve:
¼ cup white wine

Serves 4 to 6

Combine garlic, onion and olive
oil in 2-qt. casserole; cover.
Microwave at High 3 to 5
minutes, or until tender, stirring
once. Blend in water, beef
broth, mustard, thyme and
marjoram. Re-cover. Microwave
at High 30 minutes, stirring 2 or
3 times. Remove and discard
garlic. Stir in carrot. Spoon into
freezer container. Label and
freeze no longer than 1 month.

To serve, remove from
container and place in 1½-qt.
casserole; cover. Microwave at
High 9 minutes, breaking apart
and stirring 1 or 2 times. Stir in
wine. Re-cover. Microwave at
High 3 to 6 minutes, or until
heated, stirring 1 or 2 times.

Variation:
Substitute 1 can (10¾ oz.)
condensed chicken broth for
the beef broth.

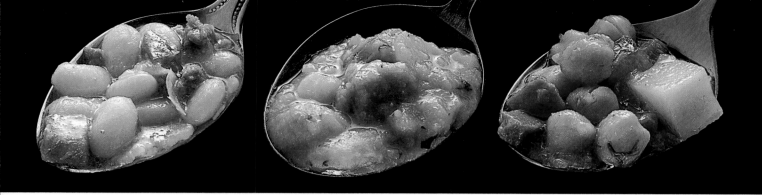

Northern Bean Soup

½ lb. ground beef, optional
8 slices bacon, cut up
1 medium onion, chopped
1 small green pepper, chopped
1 clove garlic, minced
1½ cups cubed fully cooked ham
1 lb. dried Great Northern beans, rinsed
6 cups hot water
¼ teaspoon pepper

Makes 2 soups
4 to 6 servings each

Place ground beef in 1-qt. casserole. Microwave at High 2 to 4 minutes, or until meat is no longer pink, stirring once to break apart. Drain and set aside. In 5-qt. casserole combine bacon, onion, green pepper and garlic. Microwave at High 6 to 7 minutes, or until green pepper is tender, stirring 1 or 2 times.

Stir in ground beef, ham, beans, water and pepper; cover. Microwave at High 15 to 20 minutes, or until boiling, stirring once. Reduce power to 50% (Medium). Microwave 1 to 1½ hours, or until beans are tender, stirring 3 or 4 times. Remove 1 cup beans. Mash and return to soup. Spoon into two freezer containers. Label and freeze no longer than 3 months.

To serve, remove from one container and place in 1½-qt. casserole. Microwave at High 14 to 19 minutes, or until heated, breaking apart and stirring 3 or 4 times.

Split Pea & Ham Soup

1 ham bone
6 cups hot water
1 lb. dried green split peas, rinsed
1½ cups thinly sliced carrot
1 cup chopped celery
1 cup chopped onion
1 medium red potato, peeled and finely chopped
¼ cup snipped fresh parsley
1 tablespoon instant chicken bouillon granules
¼ teaspoon pepper
⅛ teaspoon dried thyme leaves

To serve:
¼ cup half and half

Makes 2 soups
4 to 6 servings each

Combine all ingredients in 5-qt. casserole; cover. Microwave at High 1 to 1¼ hours, or until peas are tender, stirring 3 or 4 times. Remove ham bone; cool. Cut ham from bone; trim fat. Discard fat and bone. Cut ham into small pieces and return to soup. Spoon into two freezer containers. Label and freeze no longer than 3 months.

To serve, remove from one container and place in 1½-qt. casserole. Microwave at 70% (Medium-High) 15 to 25 minutes, or until heated, breaking apart and stirring 3 or 4 times. Stir in half and half.

Spanish Bean Soup

1 lb. dried garbanzo beans, rinsed
6 cups hot water
2 cups cubed fully cooked ham, ¼-in. cubes
½ lb. deep-smoked bacon, cut up
½ lb. beef flank steak, cut into thin strips
1 medium tomato, chopped
1 small green onion, chopped
1 small onion, chopped
1 medium bay leaf
¼ teaspoon ground saffron, optional
2 cups cubed peeled red potatoes, ½-in. cubes

Makes 3 soups
4 to 6 servings each

In 5-qt. casserole combine beans and hot water; cover. Microwave at High 8 to 14 minutes, or until boiling. Continue boiling at High 2 minutes. Let stand, covered, 2 hours.

Stir in remaining ingredients except potatoes; cover. Microwave at High 15 minutes. Reduce power to 50% (Medium). Microwave 2½ to 3 hours, or until beans are tender. Stir in potatoes; cover. Microwave at 50% (Medium) 20 to 30 minutes, or until potatoes are tender but not soft. Spoon into three freezer containers. Label and freeze no longer than 3 months.

To serve, remove from one container and place in 1½-qt. casserole; cover. Microwave at High 8 to 12 minutes, or until heated, breaking apart and stirring 3 or 4 times.

Chicken Rice Soup

¼ cup finely chopped green pepper
¼ cup chopped onion
1 container frozen Seasoned Chicken & Broth, below
½ cup uncooked instant rice
½ teaspoon salt
⅛ teaspoon pepper
2 drops yellow food coloring, optional

Serves 4 to 6

In 1-qt. casserole combine green pepper and onion; cover. Microwave at High 2 to 4 minutes, or until tender, stirring once. Remove stock from container and place in 2-qt. casserole; cover.

Microwave at High 15 to 22 minutes, or until boiling, breaking apart 2 or 3 times during first 10 minutes. Stir in vegetables, rice, salt, pepper and food coloring. Let stand, covered, 5 minutes.

Egg Drop Soup ▲

1 container frozen Seasoned Chicken & Broth, right
1 tablespoon soy sauce
2 drops yellow food coloring, optional
1 egg, well beaten
2 green onions, thinly sliced

Serves 4 to 6

Remove chicken and broth from container and place in 2-qt. casserole; cover. Microwave at High 15 to 22 minutes, or until boiling, stirring and breaking apart 2 or 3 times during the first 10 minutes. Mix in soy sauce and food coloring. Stir soup rapidly in circular direction, then pour egg slowly into soup. Let stand, covered, 3 minutes. Sprinkle with green onion before serving.

Seasoned Chicken & Broth

2½ to 3-lb. broiler-fryer chicken, cut into quarters
6 cups hot water
1 large carrot, cut into ½-in. pieces
1 small onion, thinly sliced
1 stalk celery with leaves, cut into 1-in. pieces
1½ teaspoons salt
¼ teaspoon dried rosemary leaves
⅛ teaspoon dried thyme leaves
5 whole peppercorns
1 bay leaf

Makes 8 cups

Place all ingredients in 5-qt. casserole; cover. Microwave at High 20 to 30 minutes, or until chicken is tender and meat near bone is no longer pink, rearranging chicken once.

Remove and discard vegetables. Remove chicken from broth; cool. Remove chicken from skin and bones. Cut into small pieces. Discard skin and bones. Skim fat from broth. Spoon chicken into two freezer containers; add broth. Label and freeze no longer than 3 months.

To serve, remove from one container and place in 1½-qt. casserole; cover. Microwave at High 12 to 16 minutes, or until heated, breaking apart and stirring 2 or 3 times.

Vegetable-Beef Soup

1½ lbs. beef boneless chuck, cut into ¾-in. cubes
2 cups cubed rutabaga, ½-in. cubes
1½ cups diagonally sliced carrots, ⅛-in. slices
1 cup thinly sliced celery
1 medium onion, cut into wedges
1 can (28 oz.) whole tomatoes, undrained, cut up
2 cups hot water
1 can (10½ oz.) condensed beef broth
1 teaspoon salt
½ teaspoon dried basil leaves
⅛ to ¼ teaspoon pepper

Makes 2 soups
4 to 6 servings each

Combine all ingredients in 3-qt. casserole; cover. Microwave at High 10 minutes. Stir. Reduce power to 50% (Medium). Microwave 1¼ to 1½ hours, or until meat and vegetables are tender, stirring 2 or 3 times. Pour into two freezer containers. Label and freeze no longer than 3 months.

To serve, remove from one container and place in 2-qt. casserole; cover. Microwave at 70% (Medium-High) 20 to 25 minutes, or until heated, breaking apart and stirring 2 or 3 times.

Beef-Barley Soup ▲

Frozen Beef & Broth, defrosted, below
2 tablespoons all-purpose flour
2 medium carrots, thinly sliced
1 small onion, thinly sliced and separated into rings
¼ cup snipped fresh parsley
2 tablespoons pearl barley
⅛ teaspoon pepper

Serves 4 to 6

Remove ½ cup broth; blend in flour. Combine remaining ingredients including beef and broth. Stir in flour mixture; cover. Microwave at High 10 minutes. Stir. Re-cover. Reduce power to 50% (Medium). Microwave 45 to 55 minutes, or until barley is tender, stirring 3 or 4 times.

Beef & Broth

3 lbs. beef shank cross cuts
5 cups hot water
2 medium carrots, cut into 1-in. pieces
2 stalks celery, cut into 1-in. pieces
1 small onion, thinly sliced
2 teaspoons salt
1 teaspoon dried bouquet garni seasoning
8 whole peppercorns

Makes 4½ to 5 cups broth and 1½ to 3 cups cut-up beef

Combine all ingredients in 5-qt. casserole; cover. Microwave at High 10 minutes. Reduce power to 50% (Medium). Microwave 1 to 1¼ hours, or until meat is fork tender, turning meat over once. Let stand 10 minutes.

Remove beef. Cool broth; skim fat. Discard vegetables. Remove bone, fat and gristle from beef; discard. Cut beef into small pieces. Wrap, label and freeze no longer than 3 months. Spoon broth into freezer container. Label and freeze no longer than 3 months.

To defrost, remove broth from container and place in 2-qt. casserole; cover. Microwave at High 12 to 15 minutes, or until heated, breaking apart and stirring 2 or 3 times. Unwrap beef and place in small bowl; cover. Microwave at High 2 to 3 minutes. Let stand 1 minute.

Meats & Main Dishes

Use the microwave-freezer team to eat well. Take advantage of supermarket specials and stock your freezer with meats. Defrost meats quickly with microwave energy for the best quality. In this section, you'll find recipes for meats microwaved from the frozen state, as well as dishes to make ahead and heat as needed.

Packaging Meats & Main Dishes

For best quality and longest freezer life, repackage meats from the market wrapped in paperboard trays and film. Some butchers will freezer-wrap meat for you on request. Choose a packaging method to suit the size and shape of the meat. You can use either freezer wraps or bags. Divide bulk quantities into meal-sized amounts. Special instructions are given below for foods which need extra preparation. To avoid freezer burn, wrap meat as airtight as possible. Cooked main dishes should be cooled before freezing. If you package in rigid plastic containers, leave head space to allow for expansion. When using a bag sealer, follow manufacturer's directions for bag size and removal of air.

Label all meats and main dishes with name of food, weight or number of servings, date of freezing and date of maximum storage time.

How to Package Meat in Freezer Paper or Foil

Cut freezer paper (coated side toward meat) or heavy-duty foil to go around meat 1½ times. Bring opposite sides together; fold over 1 inch.

Continue folding, until wrap is tight against food. Press wrap tightly against food to force out air. Make package as smooth and airtight as possible.

Crease ends of wrap to form triangles. Fold up and seal with freezer tape. Label.

How to Package Meat in Plastic Freezer Bags

Choose bag size to hold roast, single steak, chop or recipe amount of cut-up meat as manufacturer directs.

Place meat in bag. Press out as much air as possible, or use vacuum pump, if desired.

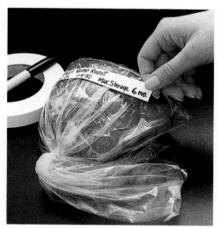

Seal with twist tie or heat sealer, as manufacturer directs. Label.

How to Package Several Steaks, Chops or Patties

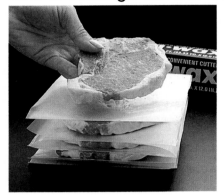

Stack servings for one meal with double thickness of wax or freezer paper between layers.

Prepare for loose-pack by arranging steaks, chops or patties on wax paper-lined tray. Freeze until firm.

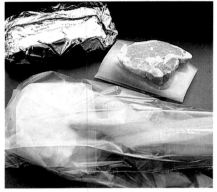

Wrap stacked or individually frozen items airtight in freezer wrap, heavy-duty foil or seal in plastic freezer bags. Label.

How to Package Ground Meat

Divide bulk ground beef into 1- to 1½-lb. portions.

Make portions no thicker than 3 inches for best defrosting.

Wrap airtight in freezer paper, heavy-duty foil or seal in plastic freezer bags. Label.

How to Package Cooked Main Dishes

Casserole. Line casserole with heavy-duty foil, leaving 1½-in. collar around edge and flattening wrinkles. Add chilled food. Freeze until firm. Remove from casserole with foil. Wrap airtight as directed on page 15.

Containers. Place chilled food in rigid plastic containers, leaving 1 inch head space in quart or ½ inch head space in pint container to allow for expansion, if necessary.

Bags. Pack and seal chilled food in heat-sealable bags as manufacturer directs. Label.

Defrosting Meats & Main Dishes

Careful defrosting is important to preserve the quality of frozen meat. The greatest dangers are moisture loss and "runaway cooking."

As meat thaws, it begins to lose some juices, but by far the greatest loss occurs after defrosting. With a microwave oven, you can defrost meat just before cooking and retain maximum moisture. Keep meat solidly frozen until you are ready to defrost. Let stand only until the center can be pierced with a skewer. The meat should still feel cold.

"Runaway cooking" occurs when the surface of the meat begins to cook before the center is defrosted. To prevent this, remove packaging before you start to defrost. The package holds juices against the surface of the meat causing the surface to cook first. Elevate roasts, steaks and chops on a rack to hold them out of their juices. If wrap sticks to the meat, you can place the wrapped package in the oven, start defrosting, and remove wrapping as soon as possible.

How to Defrost Large, Thick Roasts

Remove packaging. Place meat on roasting rack. Defrost for one-fourth total time as directed in chart, page 53.

Feel roast for warm areas. Shield these with pieces of foil. Turn roast over.

Defrost for second one-fourth total time, or until surface of meat yields to pressure.

Let stand 10 minutes. Turn roast over. Continue defrosting for additional one-fourth of time.

Shield warm areas. Turn roast over; defrost for remaining time.

Let stand 20 to 30 minutes, or until a skewer can be inserted to the center of roast.

How to Defrost Tenderloin, Flat Roasts & Large Steaks

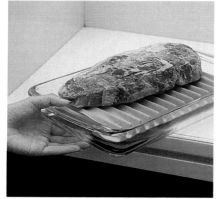

Remove packaging. Place meat on roasting rack. Defrost for half the time as directed in chart, page 53.

Shield warm areas with foil. Turn meat over. Defrost remaining time.

Let stand 5 minutes, or until a skewer can be inserted to the center of meat.

How to Defrost Small Steaks, Chops & Patties

Remove packaging. If steaks, chops or patties are stacked, separate with table knife.

Arrange meat on roasting rack. Defrost for half the time as directed in chart, page 53. Turn over and rearrange.

Defrost remaining time. Let stand 5 minutes, or until pliable.

How to Defrost Ribs

Remove packaging. Place on rack. Defrost for half the time as directed in chart, page 53. Separate ribs.

Arrange ribs with least defrosted parts to outside of dish. Defrost remaining time.

Let stand 10 to 15 minutes, or until meat is pliable.

How to Defrost Cubes & Strips

Remove packaging. Place meat in baking dish. Defrost for one-fourth total time as directed in chart, page 53, or until pieces can be separated.

Spread pieces in dish. Defrost for second one-fourth of time. Remove any defrosted pieces. Defrost remaining time, or until surface is soft.

Let stand 5 to 10 minutes, or until a skewer can be inserted to center of cubes and strips are pliable.

How to Defrost Liver Slices

Remove packaging. Place liver in baking dish. Defrost for one-third total time as directed in chart, opposite. Turn over.

Defrost for second one-third of time. Separate pieces and spread out in dish.

Defrost remaining time. Let stand 5 minutes, or until pliable.

How to Defrost Ground Meat

Remove packaging. Place meat in casserole. Defrost for one-third total time as directed in chart, opposite.

Turn meat over. Scrape off any soft pieces, if possible.

Defrost for second one-third of time. Scrape off and remove soft pieces. Set aside.

Break up remaining meat with fork. Defrost remaining time.

Check amounts over 1 pound during last one-third of time and remove defrosted meat.

Let stand 5 minutes (1 pound) to 10 minutes (over 1 pound), or until softened but still cold.

Meat Defrosting Chart

Type	Defrost Time at 50% (Medium)	Procedure
Beef		
Large Roasts	5½ - 6½ min./lb.	Follow photo directions, page 50.
Tenderloin, Flat Roasts, Large Steaks	3½ - 4½ min./lb.	Follow photo directions, page 50.
Ribs	3 - 6 min./lb.	Follow photo directions, page 51.
Liver	5 - 7 min./lb.	Follow photo directions, page 52.
Small Steaks, Chops	3 - 4 min./lb.	Follow photo directions, page 51.
Hamburgers,		
1 patty	2½ - 3½ min./lb.	Follow photo directions, page 51.
2 patties	3 - 4 min./lb.	Follow photo directions, page 51.
Cubes, Strips	3 - 5½ min./lb.	Follow photo directions, page 51.
Ground	3 - 5 min./lb.	Follow photo directions, page 52.
Pork		
Roasts	6 - 9 min./lb.	Follow photo directions, page 50.
Tenderloin	5 - 7 min./lb.	Follow photo directions, page 50.
Ribs	3 - 6 min./lb.	Follow photo directions, page 51.
Chops	3½ - 6 min./lb.	Follow photo directions, page 51.
Cubes	4 - 6 min./lb.	Follow photo directions, page 51.
Ground	3 - 5 min./lb.	Follow photo directions, page 52.
Lamb		
Roasts	5 - 8 min./lb.	Follow photo directions, page 50.
Chops	4 - 6½ min./lb.	Follow photo directions, page 51.
Cubes	4½ - 6½ min./lb.	Follow photo directions, page 51.
Ground	3 - 5 min./lb.	Follow photo directions, page 52.
Veal		
Roasts	8 - 12 min./lb.	Follow photo directions, page 50.
Round Steak	3½ - 5½ min./lb.	Follow photo directions, page 51.
Chops	4 - 6 min./lb.	Follow photo directions, page 51.
Cubes	3 - 5½ min./lb.	Follow photo directions, page 51.
Ground	3 - 5 min./lb.	Follow photo directions, page 52.

Pot Roast ▲

2½ to 3-lb. frozen beef
    chuck roast
  ⅓ cup dry sherry
  ¼ cup chili sauce
  ¼ teaspoon dry mustard
  ¼ teaspoon dried rosemary
    leaves

  ¼ teaspoon dried thyme leaves
  3 medium carrots, thinly sliced
  1 large onion, thinly sliced
  2 tablespoons all-purpose flour
  ⅓ cup cold water

Serves 4 to 6

Unwrap and place roast in 12 × 8-in. baking dish. Cover with plastic wrap. Microwave at 50% (Medium) 35 minutes. Turn over. Mix sherry, chili sauce, mustard, rosemary and thyme. Pour over roast. Place carrots and onion around roast. Cover with plastic wrap.

Microwave at 50% (Medium) 1 to 1¼ hours, or until meat is fork tender in center, rotating dish 1 or 2 times. Let stand, covered, 5 minutes. Place roast on serving platter. Cover with foil. Set aside.

Blend flour and water. Stir into vegetables in dish. Microwave at High 3½ to 6 minutes, or until thickened, stirring 2 or 3 times during cooking. Serve with meat.

Sauerbraten pictured on page 44

  3 to 3½-lb. beef tip roast

Marinade:
  2 medium carrots, shredded
  1 medium onion, sliced and
    separated into rings
  1 stalk celery, chopped
  1 cup cider vinegar
  ½ cup red wine
  ½ cup water
  2 tablespoons packed brown
    sugar
  2 teaspoons salt
10 whole peppercorns
  5 whole cloves
  1 bay leaf

To serve:
  ¼ cup all-purpose flour
  ½ cup water
  ¼ to ½ teaspoon bouquet
    sauce

Serves 6 to 8

Pierce roast generously with fork. Place in large cooking bag. In 2-qt. casserole mix all marinade ingredients; cover. Microwave at High 6 to 7 minutes, or until boiling. Pour hot marinade over roast. Seal, removing as much air as possible. Refrigerate 1 to 2 days. Place cooking bag in large freezer bag. Label and freeze no longer than 4 months.

To serve, remove roast and marinade from freezer bag and cooking bag. Place in 3-qt. casserole; cover. Microwave at High 10 minutes. Reduce power to 50% (Medium). Microwave 1¾ to 2 hours, or until tender, turning roast over 2 times.

Remove roast to platter. Cover with foil. Strain marinade; measure 1½ cups into 3-qt. casserole. Blend flour into water. Stir into marinade. Add bouquet sauce until desired color. Microwave at High 5 to 8 minutes, or until thickened, stirring 2 or 3 times. Cut roast in thin slices against the grain. Serve with gravy.

Beef Stroganoff

8 oz. fresh mushrooms, cut in
    half
1 medium onion, chopped
1 tablespoon butter or
    margarine
1½ lbs. beef top round steak,
    cut into thin strips,
    2½ × 1-in.
⅔ cup white wine
½ cup tomato juice
2 teaspoons instant beef
    bouillon granules
½ teaspoon salt
⅛ teaspoon pepper

To serve:

3 tablespoons all-purpose
    flour
⅓ cup water
½ cup dairy sour cream
1 tablespoon catsup

Serves 4 to 6

In 3-qt. casserole place
mushrooms, onion and butter;
cover. Microwave at High 4 to 8
minutes, or until onion is tender.
Stir in beef, wine, tomato juice,
bouillon granules, salt and
pepper; cover. Microwave at
High 5 minutes. Reduce power
to 50% (Medium). Microwave 22
to 29 minutes, or until beef is
tender, stirring 2 or 3 times.
Spoon into freezer container.
Label and freeze no longer than
4 months.

To serve, remove from
container and place in 2-qt.
casserole; cover. Microwave at
50% (Medium) 28 to 34
minutes, or until heated,
breaking up and stirring 2 or 3
times. With slotted spoon
remove beef to medium bowl.
Cover loosely with foil. In 1-cup
measure blend flour and water.
Stir into meat juices in casserole.
Microwave at High 5 to 8 minutes, or until thickened, stirring
2 or 3 times. Stir beef into
gravy. Mix in sour cream and
catsup. Serve over rice, page
126, or noodles, if desired.

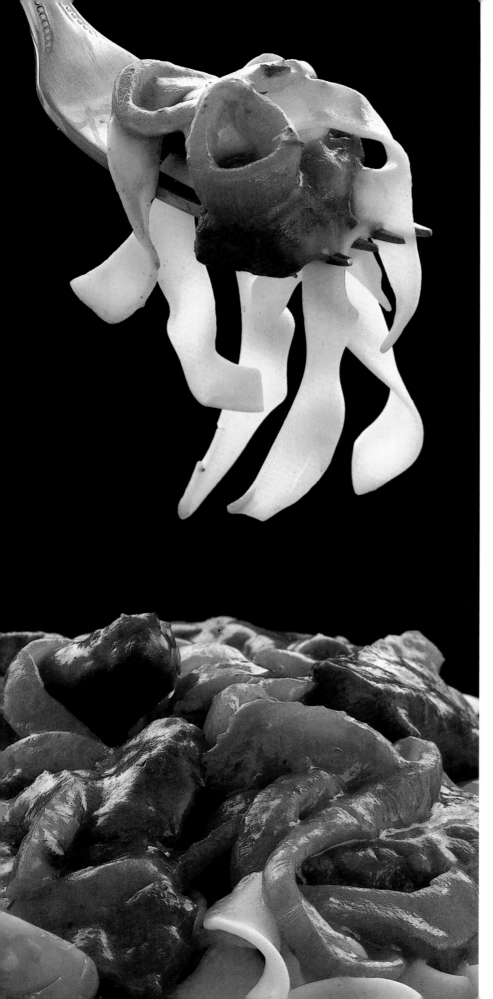

Beef Strips in Wine Sauce

- 1 medium onion, thinly sliced and separated into rings
- ⅓ cup diagonally sliced celery, ⅛-in. slices, optional
- 1 tablespoon butter or margarine
- 1½ lbs. beef boneless sirloin steak, 1-in. thick, cut into thin strips, 2 × ½-in.
- ¾ cup red wine
- 1 teaspoon instant beef bouillon granules
- 1 teaspoon dried parsley flakes
- ½ teaspoon salt
- ¼ teaspoon pepper
- ¼ teaspoon bouquet sauce

To serve:

- 2 tablespoons all-purpose flour
- ¼ cup water

Serves 4 to 6

In 2-qt. casserole combine onion, celery and butter; cover. Microwave at High 4 minutes. Stir in remaining ingredients except flour and water. Spoon into freezer container. Label and freeze no longer than 4 months.

To serve, remove from container and place in 2-qt. casserole; cover. Microwave at 70% (Medium-High) 17 to 24 minutes, or until meat is tender, stirring 2 or 3 times to break apart. Remove meat and vegetables with slotted spoon. Blend flour into water; stir into remaining liquid. Microwave at High 3½ to 5½ minutes, or until thickened. Add meat and vegetables to gravy. Serve over noodles, if desired.

Tangy Short Ribs ▶

Ribs:

- 3 lbs. beef short ribs
- ½ cup red wine
- ½ cup water
- 1 large carrot, cut into 1-in. pieces
- ¼ cup snipped fresh parsley
- 1 bay leaf
- 2 teaspoons instant beef bouillon granules
- 1½ teaspoons Worcestershire sauce
- ½ teaspoon salt
- ¼ teaspoon dried thyme leaves

Sauce:

- ½ cup chopped onion
- 1 tablespoon olive oil
- 1 cup catsup
- ⅓ cup water
- 2 tablespoons packed dark brown sugar
- 2 tablespoons lemon juice
- 2 tablespoons cider vinegar
- 1 tablespoon Worcestershire sauce
- 1 clove garlic, minced
- ¼ teaspoon celery seed
- ¼ teaspoon salt
- ¼ teaspoon pepper
- 2 drops liquid smoke, optional

Serves 4

Place ribs ingredients in 5-qt. casserole. Cover. Microwave at High 10 minutes. Rearrange and turn over ribs. Re-cover. Reduce power to 50% (Medium). Microwave 40 to 55 minutes, or until meat is tender, rearranging and turning over 2 times. Let stand, covered, 10 minutes. Drain.

In 1½-qt. casserole combine onion and olive oil. Microwave at High 3 to 5 minutes, or until onion is tender, stirring after 2 minutes. Stir in remaining sauce ingredients. Microwave at High 7 to 10 minutes, or until thickened, stirring 1 or 2 times. Place ribs in freezer container. Add sauce. Label and freeze no longer than 3 months.

To serve, remove from container and place in 3-qt. casserole; cover. Microwave at 70% (Medium-High) 20 to 25 minutes, or until heated, breaking apart and rearranging ribs 2 or 3 times. Let stand 3 to 5 minutes.

Beef Stew

- 1 tablespoon cornstarch
- ½ teaspoon salt
- ⅛ teaspoon pepper
- 1 to 1¼ lbs. beef boneless chuck roast, cut into ½-in. cubes
- 1 cup cubed rutabaga, ½-in.
- 2 cups cubed red potato, ¼-in.
- 1 can (10¾ oz.) condensed beef broth
- ½ cup thinly sliced celery
- ½ cup diagonally sliced carrot, ⅛-in. slices
- ¼ cup water
- 1 teaspoon Worcestershire sauce
- ¼ teaspoon dried basil leaves
- ⅛ teaspoon dried mint leaves

Serves 4 to 6

In 2-qt. casserole mix cornstarch, salt and pepper. Add meat, tossing to coat. Stir in remaining ingredients; cover. Microwave at High 10 minutes. Stir. Reduce power to 50% (Medium). Microwave 40 to 53 minutes, or until meat is tender, stirring 3 or 4 times. Spoon into freezer container. Label and freeze no longer than 4 months.

To serve, remove from container and place in 2-qt. casserole; cover. Microwave at 70% (Medium-High) 20 to 30 minutes, or until heated, breaking apart and stirring 2 or 3 times.

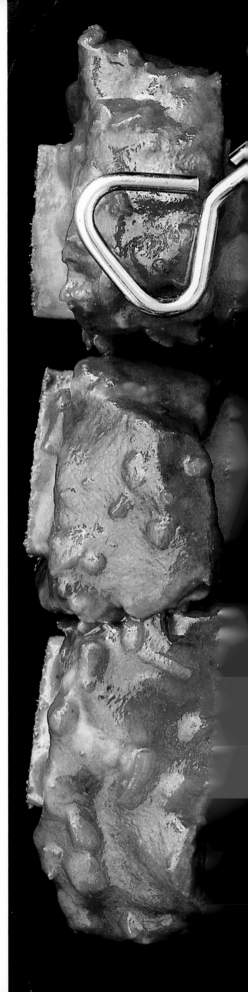

Shredded Beef Cabbage Rolls

1 head cabbage

Filling:

1½ cups sliced fresh
    mushrooms
2 cups shredded cooked
    beef
1 can (16 oz.) whole
    tomatoes, drained
    and cut up
1 cup shredded carrot
¼ cup chopped onion
1 clove garlic, minced
½ teaspoon salt
½ teaspoon dried basil
    leaves
¼ teaspoon dried rosemary
    leaves
⅛ teaspoon pepper

Sauce:

⅓ cup chopped onion
2 tablespoons olive oil
1 can (15 oz.) tomato sauce
2 tablespoons packed brown
    sugar
2 teaspoons instant beef
    bouillon granules
2 teaspoons cider vinegar
½ teaspoon dried basil
    leaves

Serves 4

How to Microwave Shredded Beef Cabbage Rolls

Cut center core from cabbage. Wrap cabbage with plastic wrap. Microwave at High 1½ to 3½ minutes, or until eight leaves can be separated easily. Remove eight leaves. Cut rib from each leaf. Set aside.

Shred 1½ cups of cabbage. Wrap and refrigerate remaining cabbage for future use. Place shredded cabbage and mushrooms in 2-qt. casserole; cover. Microwave at High 3 to 6 minutes, or until cabbage is tender, stirring after half the time. Drain.

Mix in remaining filling ingredients. Set aside. Arrange cabbage leaves on baking sheet. Cover with plastic wrap. Microwave at High 1½ to 4½ minutes, or until leaves are pliable. Spoon filling equally onto center of each leaf.

Lasagna

8 to 10 lasagna noodles
1 lb. ground beef
1 lb. bulk Italian sausage
½ cup chopped onion
1 can (15 oz.) tomato sauce
1 can (6 oz.) tomato paste
1 tablespoon packed brown
   sugar
1 clove garlic, minced
1 container (15 to 16 oz.)
   ricotta cheese

1 container (15 to 16 oz.)
   cottage cheese
½ cup grated Parmesan cheese
2 eggs, slightly beaten
½ teaspoon dried basil leaves
1 teaspoon dried parsley flakes
¼ teaspoon pepper
2 cups shredded mozzarella
   cheese, divided

Makes 2 main dishes
4 to 6 servings each

Prepare lasagna noodles as directed on package; drain. Crumble ground beef and sausage into 3-qt. casserole. Add onion. Microwave at High 7 to 8 minutes, or until meat is no longer pink, stirring 2 or 3 times to break apart. Drain. Stir in tomato sauce, tomato paste, brown sugar and garlic. Reduce power to 50% (Medium). Microwave 10 to 15 minutes, or until flavors blend, stirring every 5 minutes. Set aside.

Line two 8 × 8-in. baking dishes with freezer paper. In medium bowl mix remaining ingredients except sauce and 1 cup mozzarella cheese. Cut noodles to fit dish. Arrange one layer of noodles in each dish, then layer in each one-fourth of the cheese mixture and one-fourth of the meat sauce. Repeat with one more layer of noodles, dividing remainder of cheese mixture and sauce between dishes. Sprinkle each with ½ cup remaining mozzarella cheese. Cover with foil. Freeze until firm. Remove from dishes with freezer paper. Wrap, label and freeze no longer than 1 month.

To serve, unwrap one package and place in 8 × 8-in. baking dish. Place in oven on inverted saucer. Microwave at High 10 minutes, rotating after half the time. Reduce power to 50% (Medium). Shield corners with foil. Microwave 30 to 40 minutes, or until temperature in center reaches 140°F., rotating every 10 minutes.

Fold in sides. Roll up and secure seam with wooden picks. Place seam side down in 12 × 8-in. baking dish lined with freezer paper. Set aside. Combine onion and olive oil in medium bowl. Microwave at High 2 to 3 minutes, or until onion is tender.

Stir in remaining sauce ingredients. Microwave at High 8 to 12 minutes, or until thickened, stirring 2 or 3 times. Pour over rolls. Freeze until firm. Remove from dish with freezer paper. Wrap, label and freeze no longer than 4 months.

To serve, unwrap and place in 12 × 8-in. baking dish. Cover with plastic wrap. Microwave at High 5 minutes, rotating dish once. Reduce power to 70% (Medium-High). Microwave 22 to 28 minutes, or until heated, rearranging 2 or 3 times during cooking. Let stand 5 minutes.

◄ Tacos

1 container frozen Mexican
    Beef Mix, defrosted, left
8 taco shells
¾ cup shredded Cheddar or
    Monterey Jack cheese

Toppings:
1 medium tomato, chopped
⅓ cup chopped onion
1 cup shredded lettuce

Serves 4

Place 2 tablespoons beef mix in
each taco shell. Arrange shells
upright in paper towel-lined
8 × 8-in. baking dish. Sprinkle 2
tablespoons of cheese inside
each shell. Microwave at 70%
(Medium-High) 1½ to 2 minutes,
or until cheese melts, rotating
dish after half the time. Sprinkle
with one or all of the toppings.

◄ Mexican Pie

1 microwaved 9-in. One Crust
    Cornmeal Pastry Shell,
    page 143
1 container frozen Mexican
    Beef Mix, defrosted, left
1 can (16 oz.) refried beans
1 cup shredded Cheddar
    cheese, divided
1 cup shredded Monterey Jack
    cheese, divided

Toppings:
1 cup shredded lettuce
½ cup chopped tomato
¼ cup sliced black olives
¼ cup chopped onion
¼ cup dairy sour cream or
    salsa sauce

Serves 4 to 6

Prepare pastry shell as directed. Set aside.

Spread beans in prepared
crust. Sprinkle ½ cup of each
cheese over beans. Spread
beef mix evenly over cheese.
Top with remaining cheese.
Microwave at 50% (Medium) 6
to 10 minutes, or until heated
and cheese melts, rotating dish
1 or 2 times. Sprinkle with one
or all of the toppings.

Mexican Beef Mix

2 lbs. ground beef
½ cup chopped onion
1 tablespoon chili powder
¾ teaspoon salt
¾ teaspoon crushed red
    pepper

¼ teaspoon pepper
¼ teaspoon ground cumin
⅛ teaspoon dried oregano
    leaves
2 cloves garlic, minced

Makes 4 containers of mix

Crumble ground beef into 3-qt. casserole. Stir in onion. Microwave
at High 6 to 8 minutes, or until meat is no longer pink, stirring 2 or
3 times. Drain. Stir in remaining ingredients; cover. Reduce power
to 50% (Medium). Microwave 4 to 6 minutes, or until flavors blend,
stirring 2 or 3 times. Spoon into four freezer containers. Label and
freeze no longer than 2 months.

To defrost, remove from one container and place in 1-qt.
casserole. Microwave at 50% (Medium) 1½ to 2 minutes, or until
mixture can be broken apart. Let stand 5 to 10 minutes to
complete defrosting. Use in Tacos, Mexican Pie, Burritos or
Mexican Salad, opposite.

Mexican Salad ►

- 1 container frozen Mexican Beef Mix, defrosted, opposite
- 1 can (15 oz.) pinto beans or kidney beans, drained and rinsed
- ¼ cup French or Russian dressing
- 6 cups shredded lettuce
- 1 medium tomato, chopped
- ½ cup shredded Cheddar cheese
- ¼ cup chopped onion

Serves 6

Stir beans and dressing into defrosted beef mix. Microwave at High 1 to 2 minutes, or until heated, stirring once. Set aside. In large bowl combine remaining ingredients. Add beef and bean mixture. Toss to combine.

Burritos ►

- 1 container frozen Mexican Beef Mix, defrosted, opposite
- 4 flour tortillas, 12-in. diameter
- 1 cup chopped tomato
- 1 cup shredded lettuce
- 1 medium avocado, mashed

Serves 2 to 4

Place tortillas between damp paper towels. Microwave at High 30 to 45 seconds, or until hot to the touch. Place ¼ cup beef mix in center of each tortilla. Spoon remaining ingredients equally onto tortillas. Fold one side over filling. Fold in adjoining sides, then remaining side.

Place burritos seam side down on serving plate. Sprinkle with shredded cheese, if desired. Microwave at 70% (Medium-High) 1 to 2 minutes, or until heated and cheese melts, rotating dish ½ turn after half the cooking time. Serve with salsa sauce, if desired.

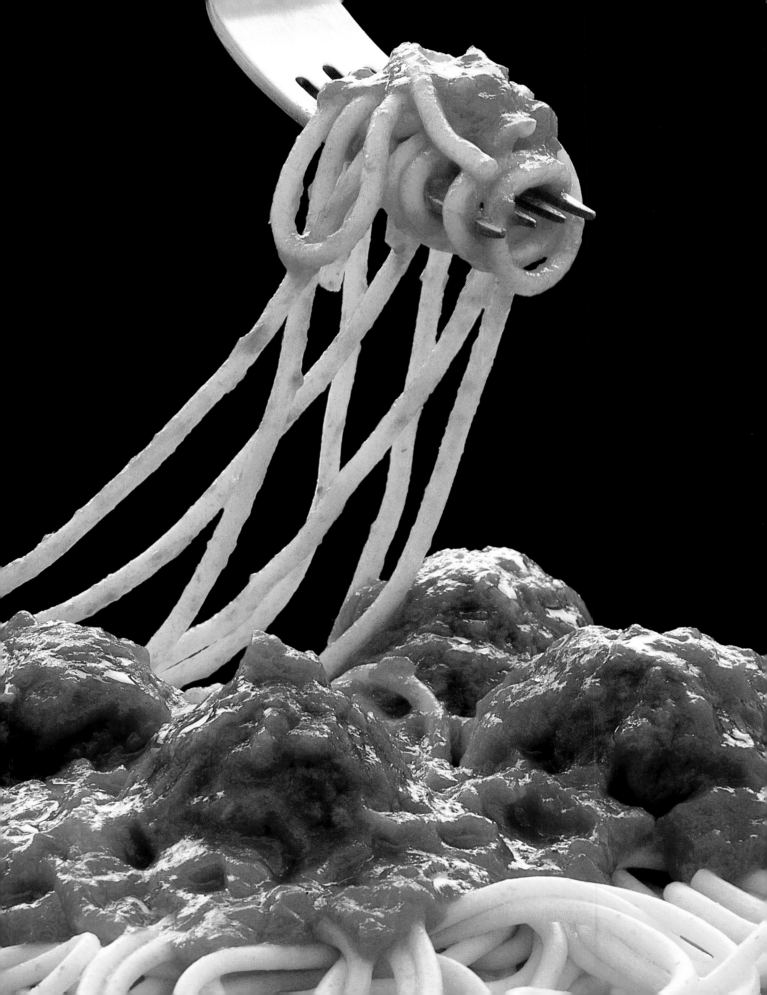

◄ Meatballs in Spaghetti Sauce

¼ cup chopped onion
1 slice bacon, cut into
   small pieces
1 can (16 oz.) whole tomatoes
1 can (6 oz.) tomato paste
1 tablespoon olive oil
1 tablespoon red wine
1 clove garlic, minced
1 bay leaf
2 teaspoons packed brown
   sugar
½ teaspoon salt
¼ teaspoon pepper
⅛ teaspoon fennel seed
1 pkg. frozen Meatballs, right

Serves 4

Place onion and bacon in 2-qt. casserole; cover. Microwave at High 1½ to 2½ minutes, or until onion is tender, stirring after half the time. Stir in remaining ingredients except meatballs. Reduce power to 50% (Medium). Microwave 10 to 15 minutes, or until flavors blend and sauce is of desired consistency, stirring 2 or 3 times.

Add frozen meatballs; cover. Microwave at 50% (Medium) 12 to 14 minutes, or until heated, stirring every 4 minutes. Let stand, covered, 5 minutes. Serve over spaghetti, if desired.

Meatballs

2 lbs. ground beef
2 eggs
½ cup dry bread crumbs
⅓ cup finely chopped onion
2 tablespoons milk
1 teaspoon salt
½ teaspoon pepper
½ teaspoon bouquet sauce
¼ teaspoon garlic powder

Makes 2 main dishes
4 servings each

Mix all ingredients in large bowl. Divide in half. Shape each half into 16 meatballs, about 2 tablespoons each. Arrange 16 meatballs in 12 × 8-in. baking dish. Microwave at High 4½ to 6 minutes, or until meatballs are firm to the touch, turning over and rearranging 2 times. Drain on paper towel. Repeat with remaining meatballs.

Arrange cooked and drained meatballs on wax paper-lined tray. Freeze until firm. Wrap in two packages. Label and freeze no longer than 2 months. Serve with Spaghetti Sauce or Sweet & Sour Sauce.

Meatballs in Sweet & Sour Sauce ▲

¼ cup cider vinegar
1 tablespoon cornstarch
1 can (15¼ oz.) crushed
   pineapple, drained
½ cup apricot preserves
⅓ cup chopped green pepper
¼ cup packed brown sugar
2 teaspoons soy sauce
⅛ teaspoon ground ginger
1 pkg. frozen Meatballs, left

Serves 4

Measure vinegar into 1-cup measure. Stir in cornstarch until smooth. Set aside. Mix remaining ingredients except meatballs in 2-qt. casserole. Stir in vinegar and cornstarch. Microwave at High 6 to 9 minutes, or until mixture is clear and thickened, stirring every 3 minutes.

Add frozen meatballs. Reduce power to 70% (Medium-High). Microwave 10 to 13 minutes, or until heated, stirring every 3 minutes. Serve over rice, page 126, if desired.

Rolled Beef Swirls

Meatloaf:

2 lbs. ground beef
2 eggs, slightly beaten
½ cup dry seasoned bread
    crumbs
¾ teaspoon salt

Filling:

2 cups sliced fresh mushrooms
¼ cup finely chopped green
    onion
¼ cup finely chopped celery
¼ cup snipped fresh parsley
2 tablespoons olive oil
1 cup shredded mozzarella
    cheese
½ cup dry seasoned bread
    crumbs
¼ cup grated Romano cheese
1 teaspoon Italian seasoning
¼ teaspoon salt
⅛ teaspoon pepper

Topping:

¼ cup sesame seed

Makes 2 main dishes
4 servings each

How to Microwave Rolled Beef Swirls

Mix meatloaf ingredients in large bowl. Set aside. In 1½-qt. casserole combine mushrooms, green onion, celery, parsley and olive oil; cover.

Microwave at High 2 to 5 minutes, or until vegetables are tender-crisp. Stir in remaining filling ingredients. Set aside.

Place sesame seed in 9-in. pie plate. Microwave at High 5 to 8 minutes, or until sesame seed turns light brown, stirring after every 2 minutes.

Pat meatloaf mixture into 15×9-in. rectangle on wax paper. Sprinkle evenly with cheese filling. Roll up tightly from short side by lifting paper. Continue lifting paper and rolling until completely rolled up.

Roll in sesame seed, pressing to coat. Cut into eight equal pieces. Place on wax paper-lined tray. Freeze until firm. Wrap in two packages. Label and freeze no longer than 2 months.

To serve, unwrap one package and place on roasting rack. Cover with wax paper. Micro-wave at 70% (Medium-High) 18 to 22 minutes, or until set, rotating rack 1 or 2 times. Let stand 3 minutes.

65

Stuffed Green Peppers ▲

4 large green peppers

Stuffing:
1 lb. lean ground beef
1 can (7½ oz.) whole tomatoes
½ cup uncooked instant rice
½ cup frozen corn
¼ cup grated Parmesan
    cheese
2 tablespoons finely chopped
    onion

1 tablespoon chopped
    pimiento, optional
½ teaspoon celery salt
⅛ teaspoon garlic powder
⅛ teaspoon pepper

To serve:
1 container frozen Tomato
    Sauce, defrosted,
    page 123*

Serves 4

Cut tops off green peppers; core and remove seeds. Place cut side up on wax paper-lined tray. In medium bowl mix all stuffing ingredients. Spoon stuffing into green peppers. Freeze until firm. Wrap individually. Label and freeze no longer than 1 month.

To serve, unwrap four stuffed green peppers and arrange upright in 8 × 8-in. baking dish, or in four individual dishes. Cover with plastic wrap. Microwave at High 3 minutes. Reduce power to 70% (Medium-High). Microwave 28 to 35 minutes, or until stuffing is set, rearranging peppers 2 or 3 times. Let stand, covered, 5 minutes. Defrost frozen sauce as directed, then microwave at High 4 to 6 minutes, or until heated. Serve over green peppers.

*Substitute 1 can (8 oz.) tomato sauce plus ¼ teaspoon sugar, ⅛ teaspoon basil leaves and ⅛ teaspoon onion powder. Combine in small bowl.

Chili

2 lbs. ground beef
2 medium onions, chopped
2 cans (16 oz. each) whole
    tomatoes
2 cans (15½ oz. each) kidney
    beans
2 cans (10¾ oz. each) tomato
    soup
1 to 2 tablespoons chili
    powder
1 tablespoon ground cumin
1 tablespoon paprika
1½ to 2 teaspoons crushed red
    pepper
1 teaspoon salt
1 teaspoon sugar

Makes 2 main dishes
4 to 6 servings each

Crumble ground beef into 5-qt. casserole. Add onions; cover. Microwave at High 6 to 8 minutes, or until meat is no longer pink, stirring 2 or 3 times during cooking. Drain.

Stir in remaining ingredients; cover. Microwave at High 10 minutes. Stir. Reduce power to 70% (Medium-High). Microwave, uncovered, 25 to 35 minutes, or until slightly thickened. Spoon into two freezer containers. Label and freeze no longer than 4 months.

To serve, unwrap one container and place in 2-qt. casserole; cover. Microwave at 70% (Medium-High) 17 to 26 minutes, or until heated, breaking apart with fork as soon as possible and stirring 1 or 2 times. Top chili with finely chopped onion, shredded Cheddar cheese and chopped tomatoes, if desired.

Cuban Hash

2 lbs. ground beef
1 medium onion, chopped
1 small green pepper,
   chopped
2 cloves garlic, minced
2 tablespoons olive oil
1 can (16 oz.) whole tomatoes
1 can (6 oz.) tomato paste
¾ cup hot water
¼ cup red wine
⅓ cup raisins, optional
1 bottle (3 oz.) capers, drained
1 small bay leaf
1 tablespoon red wine vinegar
2 teaspoons dried oregano
   leaves
2 teaspoons packed brown
   sugar
½ teaspoon salt

Makes 2 main dishes
4 to 6 servings each

Crumble ground beef into 3-qt. casserole. Microwave at High 6 to 8 minutes, or until no longer pink, stirring 1 or 2 times. Drain and set aside.

In medium bowl combine onion, green pepper, garlic and olive oil. Microwave at High 2 to 4 minutes, or until tender, stirring once. Stir vegetables and remaining ingredients into ground beef. Microwave at High 30 to 35 minutes, or until thickened, stirring 2 or 3 times. Spoon loosely into two freezer containers. Label and freeze no longer than 6 months.

To serve, remove from one container and place in 1-qt. casserole. Cover with plastic wrap. Microwave at High 10 to 15 minutes, or until heated, breaking apart and stirring 3 or 4 times during cooking. Serve over rice, page 126, if desired.

◄ Rolled Pork Roast With Sweet Potatoes

½ cup packed brown sugar
1 tablespoon cornstarch
¾ cup orange juice
¼ cup pineapple preserves
⅛ teaspoon salt

3 lb. frozen pork boneless
   rolled loin roast
1 can (23 oz.) sweet potatoes,
   drained

Serves 6 to 8

In 1-qt. casserole mix brown sugar and cornstarch. Stir in orange juice, pineapple preserves and salt. Microwave at High 3 to 5 minutes, or until thickened, stirring after every minute. Cover and set aside.

Unwrap frozen roast and place on roasting rack. Cover with wax paper. Microwave at 50% (Medium) 25 minutes. Turn roast over. Brush lightly with glaze; cover. Microwave at 50% (Medium) 20 minutes. Add potatoes. Brush meat and potatoes lightly with glaze. Microwave, uncovered, at 50% (Medium) 12 to 25 minutes, or until internal temperature reaches 165°F. when checked in several places, rotating once during cooking. Let stand, covered with foil, 10 minutes. Brush with any remaining glaze.

Pork Loaf ►

1 cup shredded zucchini
1 cup sliced fresh mushrooms
¼ cup grated Parmesan
   cheese
1 teaspoon Italian seasoning
¼ teaspoon garlic powder
¼ teaspoon pepper

1 lb. ground pork
½ lb. bulk hot Italian sausage
2 tablespoons butter or
   margarine
⅓ cup dry seasoned bread
   crumbs
½ teaspoon paprika

Serves 4 to 6

Place zucchini and mushrooms in small bowl. Microwave at High 2 minutes. Drain. Stir in cheese, Italian seasoning, garlic powder and pepper. Set aside.

In medium bowl mix pork and sausage. Place on large piece of wax paper. Press into 15 × 7-in. rectangle. Sprinkle with zucchini-mushroom mixture. Roll up tightly from short side by lifting paper and rolling until completely rolled up. Smooth seam and sides.

Place butter in small bowl. Microwave at High 30 to 45 seconds, or until butter melts. In pie plate or on wax paper mix bread crumbs with paprika. Brush pork loaf with melted butter, then coat with crumbs. Place on wax paper-lined tray. Freeze until firm. Wrap, label and freeze no longer than 2 months.

To serve, unwrap and place on roasting rack. Cover with wax paper. Microwave at High 3 minutes. Reduce power to 50% (Medium). Microwave 36 to 41 minutes, or until internal temperature reaches 165° F. when checked in several places, rotating rack 4 or 5 times during cooking. Shield ends with foil during last half of cooking time, if necessary.

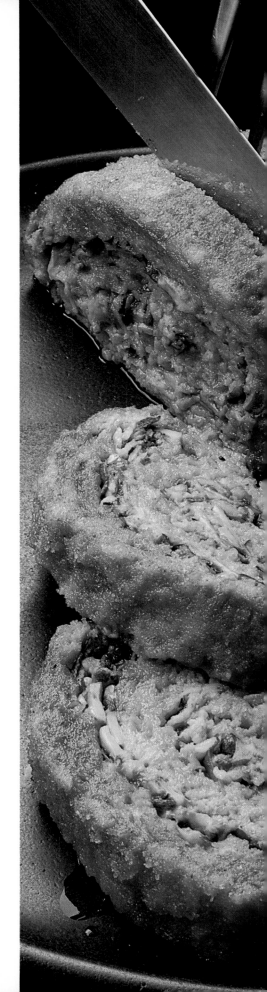

◄ Grilled Ribs

3 lbs. fresh pork spareribs, cut
   into 2 or 3 sections
¾ cup hot water
1 small onion, sliced and
   separated into rings
¼ teaspoon dried thyme leaves

Sauce:
½ cup soy sauce
⅓ cup packed brown sugar
2 tablespoons dry sherry
2 tablespoons chopped
   crystallized ginger
1 teaspoon five spice powder
1 teaspoon salt

Serves 3 to 4

In 3- to 5-qt. casserole combine ribs, water, onion and thyme; cover. Microwave at High 5 minutes. Reduce power to 50% (Medium). Microwave 45 minutes to 1¼ hours, or until ribs are tender, rearranging 2 or 3 times during cooking. Let stand, covered, 5 to 10 minutes.

In medium bowl mix all sauce ingredients. Microwave at High 2 to 4 minutes, or until sugar dissolves, stirring 1 or 2 times.

Place ribs on charcoal grill over medium-hot coals. Brush with sauce. Grill 15 to 30 minutes, or until sauce is set, brushing with additional sauce and turning ribs over 2 or 3 times. Cool. Place on wax paper-lined tray. Freeze until firm. Wrap, label and freeze no longer than 2 months.

To serve, unwrap and place on baking sheet. Cover with wax paper. Microwave at 70% (Medium-High) 8 to 13 minutes, or until heated, rearranging 1 or 2 times.

Variation:
Grilled Barbecued Ribs: Prepare as directed except substitute 1 cup prepared barbecue sauce for the sauce ingredients.

Pork Roast With Gravy

3 lb. frozen pork loin roast
1 envelope (¾ oz.) brown or
   pork gravy mix
1 cup water, divided

⅛ teaspoon dried thyme leaves
   Dash pepper
1 tablespoon all-purpose flour

Serves 4 to 6

Unwrap and place frozen roast fat side down in shallow 3-qt. casserole. Cover with plastic wrap. Microwave at 50% (Medium) 40 minutes. Drain and discard liquid.

In small bowl blend gravy mix, ¾ cup water, thyme and pepper. Turn roast fat side up. Pour gravy mixture over roast; cover. Microwave at 50% (Medium) 25 to 35 minutes, or until internal temperature reaches 165°F. when checked in several places, rotating casserole once during cooking. Remove roast to serving plate. Cover with foil. Let stand 5 to 10 minutes.

In 1-cup measure blend remaining ¼ cup water and the flour. Blend into gravy mix in casserole until smooth. Microwave at High 2 to 5 minutes, or until thickened, stirring with fork or wire whip 1 or 2 times. Serve with roast.

Pork Chops Stroganoff

2 cups sliced fresh mushrooms
1 medium onion, thinly sliced
    and separated into rings
1 clove garlic, minced
2 tablespoons butter or
    margarine
¼ cup water
½ teaspoon salt
⅛ teaspoon pepper
1 small bay leaf
4 butterflied pork chops, 1-in.
    thick (about 1½ lbs.)

To serve:
2 tablespoons all-purpose flour
¼ cup white wine
½ cup dairy sour cream

Serves 4

In 1-qt. casserole place mushrooms, onion, garlic and butter. Microwave at High 3 to 5 minutes, or until tender. Stir in water, salt, pepper and bay leaf.

Arrange chops in 12 × 8-in. foil-lined baking dish. Pour mushroom mixture over chops. Freeze until firm. Remove from dish with foil. Wrap, label and freeze no longer than 4 months.

To serve, unwrap and place in 12 × 8-in. baking dish. Cover with wax paper. Microwave at High 5 minutes, rotating dish ½ turn after half the time, breaking sauce apart and turning chops over. Re-cover. Reduce power to 70% (Medium-High). Microwave 26 to 31 minutes, or until internal temperature reaches 170°F. when checked in several places, rearranging chops 2 or 3 times and turning over once. Place chops on serving plate; cover.

Blend flour and wine; stir into mushroom sauce. Increase power to High. Microwave 1 to 3 minutes, or until thickened, blending with fork 1 or 2 times. Blend in sour cream. Reduce power to 50% (Medium). Microwave 1 to 2 minutes, or until sauce is heated. Serve over pork chops.

Stuffed Pork Chops

3 Corn Muffins, page 133
¼ cup thinly sliced celery
¼ cup chopped apple
1 tablespoon finely chopped
   onion
¼ cup butter or margarine
1 cup soft bread cubes, ½-in.
3 tablespoons raisins
⅛ teaspoon ground sage
⅛ teaspoon salt
   Dash pepper
4 butterflied pork chops, 1-in.
   thick (about 1½ lbs.)

Serves 4

How to Microwave Stuffed Pork Chops

Prepare corn muffins as directed. Crumble in small bowl; set aside.

Combine celery, apple, onion and butter in 1-qt. casserole. Microwave at High 45 seconds to 1½ minutes, or until tender. Stir in crumbs and remaining ingredients except pork chops.

Pork Stew

1 medium red potato, cut into ¼-in. cubes
1 medium carrot, thinly sliced
½ cup thinly sliced celery
2 tablespoons butter or margarine
1 medium zucchini, sliced into 2 × ½-in. strips
2 tablespoons snipped fresh parsley
1 can (16 oz.) whole tomatoes, cut up, undrained

2 cups cubed cooked pork, ½-in. cubes
1 teaspoon instant beef bouillon granules
½ teaspoon sugar
½ teaspoon salt
¼ teaspoon dried rosemary leaves
¼ teaspoon pepper

To serve:
2 tablespoons all-purpose flour
¼ cup white wine

Serves 4

Combine potato, carrot, celery and butter in medium bowl; cover. Microwave at High 3 to 5 minutes, or until vegetables are still crisp and colors brighten, stirring once. Add zucchini and parsley. Re-cover. Microwave at High 2 to 3 minutes, or until zucchini is hot and tender-crisp. Stir in tomatoes with liquid, pork, bouillon granules, sugar, salt, rosemary and pepper. Spoon into freezer container. Label and freeze no longer than 2 months.

To serve, remove from container and place in 1½-qt. casserole; cover. Microwave at High 5 minutes. Reduce power to 70% (Medium-High). Microwave 4 to 8 minutes, or until defrosted but still cold, breaking apart with fork as soon as possible.

Drain ¾ cup liquid into 2-cup measure. Blend in flour. Stir in wine. Microwave at High 2½ to 5 minutes, or until thickened, stirring after every minute. Stir sauce into stew; cover. Reduce power to 70% (Medium-High). Microwave 8 to 12 minutes, or until heated, stirring 2 or 3 times during cooking. Serve over rice, page 126, if desired.

Arrange chops on wax paper-lined tray. Spoon stuffing onto each pork chop. Freeze until firm. Wrap, label and freeze no longer than 4 months.

To serve, unwrap and place chops on roasting rack; cover with wax paper. Microwave at High 5 minutes. Rearrange chops. Re-cover. Reduce power to 50% (Medium). Microwave 16 to 22 minutes, or until meat is no longer pink and internal temperature reaches 170°F., rearranging chops 2 or 3 times. Let stand, covered, 5 minutes.

Pork & Vegetables ▲

2 lbs. pork boneless shoulder blade roast, cut into ¾-in. cubes
2 cups diagonally sliced carrots, ⅛-in. slices
2 cups diagonally sliced celery, ⅛-in. slices
1 can (14½ oz.) chicken broth
½ cup white wine
3 slices lemon rind
1 tablespoon instant minced onion
½ teaspoon dried savory leaves
½ teaspoon dried marjoram leaves
½ teaspoon bouquet sauce
⅛ teaspoon garlic powder
⅛ teaspoon pepper
1 bay leaf
2 medium green peppers, sliced

To serve:

1 tablespoon plus 1 teaspoon all-purpose flour

Makes 2 main dishes
4 to 6 servings each

Place pork cubes in 3-qt. casserole. Microwave at High 5 minutes, stirring once. Drain. Add remaining ingredients except green peppers and flour; cover. Reduce power to 50% (Medium). Microwave 45 to 60 minutes, or until meat and vegetables are tender, stirring 3 or 4 times during cooking. Add green peppers during last 5 to 10 minutes of cooking. Remove lemon rind and bay leaf. Spoon into two freezer containers. Label and freeze no longer than 2 months.

To serve, remove from one container and place in 1-qt. casserole; cover. Microwave at High 5 minutes. Break apart with fork. Reduce power to 70% (Medium-High). Re-cover. Microwave 2 to 5 minutes, or until defrosted but still cold, stirring once.

Drain ⅔ cup liquid from casserole into 2-cup measure. Blend in flour. Microwave at High 2 to 4½ minutes, or until thickened, stirring after every minute. Stir sauce into casserole. Re-cover. Reduce power to 70% (Medium-High). Microwave 3 to 7 minutes, or until heated, stirring 1 or 2 times.

Pork-Parmesan Rice

4 cups cooked brown rice, page 126
3 tablespoons butter or margarine
1 medium green pepper, cut into 1½ × ¼-in. strips
2 cups cubed cooked pork, ¼-in. cubes
1 cup grated Parmesan cheese
1 jar (2 oz.) chopped pimientos, drained, optional
1 teaspoon onion salt
¼ teaspoon dried basil leaves
¼ teaspoon dried marjoram leaves
⅛ teaspoon pepper
Paprika

Makes 2 main dishes
4 to 6 servings each

Prepare rice as directed. Let stand. Place butter in small bowl. Microwave at High 30 to 45 seconds, or until butter melts. Mix butter and remaining ingredients into rice in casserole. Spoon into two freezer containers. Label and freeze no longer than 1 month.

To serve, remove from one container and place in 1-qt. casserole; cover. Microwave at 50% (Medium) 2½ to 4 minutes, or until rice can be broken apart with fork. Re-cover. Increase power to High. Microwave 5 to 7 minutes, or until very hot and cheese melts, stirring 2 or 3 times. Sprinkle with paprika.

Fruited Pork

½ cup water
¼ cup cider vinegar
2 tablespoons light molasses
1 tablespoon soy sauce
    Dash pepper
1 lb. pork boneless loin roast,
    cut into thin strips, 2 × ¼-in.
1 medium apple, chopped
⅓ cup chopped walnuts
⅓ cup raisins

To serve:
1 can (11 oz.) mandarin
    orange sections, drained
    and ¼ cup juice reserved
1 tablespoon plus 2 teaspoons
    cornstarch

Serves 4 to 6

In 2-qt. casserole mix water,
vinegar, molasses, soy sauce
and pepper. Microwave at High
1 to 2½ minutes, or until
blended, stirring after half the
time. Stir in pork; cover. Marinate
1 hour at room temperature.

Drain, reserving 2 tablespoons
marinade. Microwave, uncovered, at 70% (Medium-High) 3
to 6 minutes, or until meat is no
longer pink, stirring after half the
time. Add reserved marinade,
apple, walnuts and raisins.
Spoon into freezer container.
Label and freeze no longer than
2 months.

To serve, remove from
container and place in 2-qt.
casserole; cover. Microwave at
70% (Medium-High) 11 to 17
minutes, or until heated,
breaking apart and stirring 2 or
3 times. Drain liquid into 4-cup
measure. Stir orange sections
into casserole; cover. Let stand.
Blend cornstarch and ¼ cup
reserved juice. Stir into liquid in
4-cup measure. Microwave at
High 2 to 3 minutes, or until
thickened, stirring 3 or 4 times.
Mix into casserole. Serve over
rice, page 126, if desired.

Broccoli-Stuffed Ham

2 cups chopped fresh broccoli
2 cups sliced fresh mushrooms
¼ cup chopped celery
½ cup dry seasoned bread
   crumbs
½ cup shredded Colby cheese
⅓ cup ricotta cheese
½ teaspoon onion salt
¼ teaspoon pepper
8 thin slices fully cooked ham

To serve:

1 tablespoon butter or
   margarine
1 tablespoon all-purpose flour
⅔ cup milk
1 tablespoon snipped fresh
   parsley
1 teaspoon grated onion
¼ teaspoon salt
½ cup shredded Monterey Jack
   cheese
2 teaspoons prepared mustard

Makes 2 main dishes
4 servings each

In 1½-qt. casserole combine broccoli, mushrooms and celery; cover. Microwave at High 4½ to 6½ minutes, or until tender-crisp, stirring 1 or 2 times. Stir in bread crumbs, cheeses, onion salt and pepper.

Spread about ¼ cup on each ham slice. Roll up and secure with wooden pick. Wrap individually. Label and freeze no longer than 2 months.

To serve, unwrap four roll-ups and arrange in 8 × 8-in. baking dish. Cover with wax paper. Microwave at 50% (Medium) 11 to 17 minutes, or until stuffing is heated, turning over once and rearranging 1 or 2 times. Let stand 3 to 5 minutes.

Place butter in 4-cup measure. Microwave at High 30 to 45 seconds, or until butter melts. Blend in flour, then milk. Stir in parsley, onion and salt. Micro-wave at High 2 to 3½ minutes, or until thickened, stirring 1 or 2 times. Add cheese and mustard, stirring until cheese melts. Serve over roll-ups.

Ham Meatballs ▲

1 lb. ground ham
½ lb. ground pork
½ cup dry bread crumbs
2 eggs, slightly beaten
2 tablespoons chopped onion
2 tablespoons milk
1 tablespoon brown mustard
¼ teaspoon pepper

Serves 4 to 6

Mix all ingredients in medium bowl. Shape by tablespoonfuls into two dozen 1½- to 2-in. balls. Arrange on wax paper-lined tray. Freeze until firm. Wrap, label and freeze no longer than 2 months.

To serve, unwrap and arrange in 12 × 8-in. baking dish. Cover with wax paper. Microwave at High 14 to 18 minutes, or until set, turning over and rearranging 3 or 4 times. Let stand 3 to 5 minutes. Serve meatballs with Apple-Raisin Glaze or Mustard Sauce, right.

Apple-Raisin Glaze ▲

¼ cup packed brown sugar
2 teaspoons cornstarch
⅔ cup apple cider
1 teaspoon lemon juice
¼ cup raisins
⅛ teaspoon ground cinnamon

Makes 1 cup

In 4-cup measure or bowl mix brown sugar and cornstarch. Stir in remaining ingredients. Microwave at High 2 to 3 minutes, or until thickened, stirring 2 or 3 times. Serve over Ham Meatballs, left.

Mustard Sauce

2 tablespoons butter or margarine
2 tablespoons all-purpose flour
1 cup half and half
1 tablespoon Dijon-style mustard
⅛ teaspoon dry mustard
1 egg yolk, slightly beaten
1 tablespoon snipped fresh parsley
¼ teaspoon red wine vinegar

Makes 1 cup

Place butter in 4-cup measure. Microwave at High 30 to 45 seconds, or until butter melts. Stir in flour. Blend in half and half, Dijon-style mustard and dry mustard. Microwave at 50% (Medium) 4½ to 6 minutes, or until thickened, stirring with wire whip after the first 2 minutes and then after every minute. Stir small amount of hot mixture into beaten egg yolk. Return to hot mixture, stirring constantly. Mix in remaining ingredients. Microwave at 50% (Medium) 1 minute. Stir. Serve with Ham Meatballs, left.

Moussaka

Filling:
 1 lb. ground lamb
½ lb. ground beef
 1 can (16 oz.) whole tomatoes, drained and chopped
 3 cups chopped zucchini
 1 can (6 oz.) tomato paste
¼ cup red wine
 2 tablespoons water
 1 tablespoon olive oil
 1 tablespoon minced onion
 1 clove garlic, minced
 1 teaspoon dried basil leaves
½ teaspoon dried oregano leaves
½ teaspoon ground cinnamon
½ teaspoon salt
¼ teaspoon pepper

Vegetable:
 4 cups water

 1 tablespoon salt
 1 eggplant, peeled and sliced ½ inch thick (about 1½ lbs.)
 1 cup hot water
 1 teaspoon instant beef bouillon granules

Topping:
 1 tablespoon butter or margarine
 1 tablespoon cornstarch
 1 teaspoon dried parsley flakes
¼ teaspoon salt
⅛ teaspoon pepper
 1 cup milk
 1 egg, slightly beaten
 1 cup ricotta cheese
 2 tablespoons grated Parmesan cheese

Makes 2 main dishes
4 to 6 servings each

Crumble lamb and beef into 3-qt. casserole; cover. Microwave at High 4½ to 6½ minutes, or until meat is no longer pink, stirring once. Drain. Stir in remaining filling ingredients. Reduce power to 70% (Medium-High). Microwave, uncovered, 25 to 30 minutes, or until filling is thickened and zucchini is tender, stirring 3 or 4 times during cooking. Set aside.

In large bowl combine 4 cups water and 1 tablespoon salt. Add eggplant slices. Soak 5 minutes. Drain. Pat dry with paper towels. Add hot water and bouillon granules to eggplant in bowl. Cover with plastic wrap. Microwave at High 12 to 16 minutes, or until eggplant is tender, rearranging and turning over slices 1 or 2 times. Divide and arrange eggplant slices in two 8 × 8-in. foil-lined baking dishes. Divide filling between dishes; spread over eggplant. Set aside.

Place butter in 4-cup measure. Microwave at High 30 to 45 seconds, or until butter melts. Stir in cornstarch, parsley, salt and pepper. Blend in milk. Microwave at High 3 to 5 minutes, or until thickened, stirring after every minute. Stir small amount of hot mixture into beaten egg. Return to hot mixture, stirring constantly. Microwave at High 30 to 45 seconds, or until thick. Stir in ricotta and Parmesan cheese. Divide cheese mixture and spread over filling. Freeze until firm. Remove from dishes with foil. Wrap, label and freeze no longer than 1 month.

To serve, unwrap one package and place in 8 × 8-in. baking dish. Shield corners with foil. Cover with wax paper. Place dish on saucer. Microwave at High 5 minutes. Rotate ½ turn. Reduce power to 50% (Medium). Microwave 10 minutes. Remove shields and rotate dish. Cover with wax paper. Microwave at 50% (Medium) 27 to 34 minutes, or until center is heated, rotating dish 2 or 3 times. Let stand 5 minutes.

Lamb Stew

3 tablespoons cornstarch
½ teaspoon salt
½ teaspoon pepper
2½ lbs. lamb boneless shoulder,
    cut into ½-in. cubes
2 potatoes, peeled and cut
    into 1-in. cubes
2 medium carrots, cut into
    1-in. pieces
1 large onion, cut into 2-in.
    pieces
1½ cups hot water
2 tablespoons snipped fresh
    parsley
1 tablespoon instant beef
    bouillon granules
2 bay leaves
½ teaspoon bouquet sauce
2 medium apples, cored and
    diced
1 pkg. (10 oz.) frozen peas

Makes 2 main dishes
4 to 6 servings each

Place cornstarch, salt and pepper in 5-qt. casserole. Add lamb, tossing to coat. Stir in remaining ingredients except apples and peas; cover. Microwave at High 10 minutes. Stir. Reduce power to 50% (Medium). Microwave, covered, 30 minutes, stirring every 10 minutes. Add apples and peas. Microwave, covered, 15 to 30 minutes, or until meat and vegetables are tender, stirring 2 or 3 times. Spoon into two freezer containers. Label and freeze no longer than 4 months.

To serve, remove from one container and place in 2-qt. casserole. Cover. Microwave at 70% (Medium-High) 20 to 28 minutes, or until heated, breaking apart as soon as possible and stirring 3 or 4 times during cooking.

Mediterranean Lamb With Couscous ▲

1 large onion, chopped
3 tablespoons olive oil
2½ lbs. lamb boneless shoulder,
    cut into ½-in. cubes
6 medium carrots, thinly
    sliced
4 cups sliced zucchini
1 large green pepper, cut into
    thin strips
1 can (28 oz.) whole tomatoes,
    drained and cut up
1 can (15 oz.) garbanzo
    beans, rinsed and drained
1 can (10½ oz.) condensed
    beef broth

1 can (6 oz.) tomato paste
1 teaspoon crushed red
    pepper
½ teaspoon ground cumin
½ teaspoon salt
½ teaspoon ground coriander
¼ teaspoon pepper

To serve:
2 cups hot water
1 tablespoon instant chicken
    bouillon granules
2 cups cooked medium
    grain couscous

Makes 2 main dishes
4 to 6 servings each

Place onion and olive oil in 5-qt. casserole. Microwave at High 5 to 7 minutes, or until tender. Stir in remaining ingredients except water, bouillon granules and couscous; cover.

Microwave at High 10 minutes. Reduce power to 50% (Medium). Microwave 1 to 1¼ hours, or until meat and vegetables are tender, stirring 2 or 3 times. Spoon into two freezer containers. Label and freeze no longer than 4 months.

To serve, remove from one container and place in 2-qt. casserole. Cover. Microwave at 70% (Medium-High) 32 to 37 minutes, or until heated, breaking apart as soon as possible, then stirring 2 or 3 times. Let stand, covered.

In 1-qt. casserole combine water and bouillon granules; cover. Microwave at High 1½ to 3½ minutes, or until water boils. Stir in couscous. Let stand, covered, 5 to 10 minutes, or until tender. Arrange couscous on large serving platter. Top with lamb mixture.

Spicy Pizza Pie

1 microwaved 9-in. One Crust
Whole Wheat Pastry Shell,
page 143
1 medium green pepper, cut
into 2 × ¼-in. strips
½ lb. chorizo sausage, cut into
½-in. slices
¼ cup sliced pepperoni
1 can (8 oz.) tomato sauce
1 cup sliced fresh mushrooms
½ teaspoon chili powder
⅛ teaspoon ground cumin
⅛ teaspoon dried oregano
leaves
2 tablespoons sliced pitted
black olives
⅓ cup shredded mozzarella
cheese
⅓ cup shredded Cheddar
cheese

Serves 4 to 6

Prepare pastry shell as directed.
Set aside. Place green pepper
in small bowl. Cover with plastic
wrap. Microwave at High 30
seconds to 1½ minutes, or until
tender-crisp. Set aside.

In 1-qt. casserole combine
chorizo sausage and pepperoni.
Cover with wax paper. Microwave at High 3 to 5 minutes, or
until chorizo is firm, stirring 1 or
2 times. Drain and set aside. In
4-cup measure or bowl mix
tomato sauce, mushrooms and
seasonings. Microwave at High
5 to 8 minutes, or until
thickened, stirring 2 or 3 times.

Stir sausage, pepperoni, green
pepper and olives into sauce.
Pour into pie shell. Sprinkle with
mozzarella and Cheddar
cheese. Wrap, label and freeze
no longer than 2 months.

To serve, unwrap and cover pie
with wax paper. Microwave at
High 3 minutes. Rotate ½ turn.
Reduce power to 50%
(Medium). Microwave 21 to 28
minutes, or until heated in
center, rotating 4 or 5 times. Let
stand 5 to 10 minutes.

Hearty Simmered Sausage

6 slices bacon, cut up
2 lbs. Polish sausage, cut into
    1-in. pieces
4 cups cubed red potatoes,
    ½-in. cubes
1 can (14½ oz.) chicken broth
1 cup vermouth
1 cup chopped Canadian
    bacon or fully cooked ham
1 cup sliced pepperoni
1 medium onion, thinly sliced
    and separated into rings
⅓ cup chopped carrot
1 clove garlic, minced
1 teaspoon dried bouquet
    garni seasoning

> Makes 2 main dishes
> 4 to 6 servings each

Place cut-up bacon in 5-qt. casserole; cover. Microwave at High 6 to 8 minutes, or until crisp, stirring once. Stir in remaining ingredients; cover.

Microwave at High 10 minutes. Reduce power to 70% (Medium-High). Microwave 35 to 40 minutes, or until potatoes are tender, stirring 2 or 3 times during cooking. Skim fat. Spoon into two freezer containers. Label and freeze no longer than 2 months.

To serve, remove from one container and place in 2-qt. casserole. Cover. Microwave at 70% (Medium-High) 21 to 29 minutes, or until hot, breaking apart as soon as possible and stirring 3 or 4 times.

Cassoulet ▲

2 lbs. dried Great Northern
    beans
8 cups hot water
2 teaspoons salt
¼ lb. pork boneless loin roast,
    cut into 1-in. cubes
1 cup chopped onion, divided
½ teaspoon garlic powder
1 can (28 oz.) whole tomatoes,
    drained
¼ cup white wine
2 teaspoons dried parsley
    flakes

¼ teaspoon pepper
12 oz. Polish sausage,
    cut into 1-in. pieces
2 slices bacon, cut into ½-in.
    pieces
1 tablespoon plus 1½
    teaspoons instant chicken
    bouillon granules
½ teaspoon dried bouquet
    garni seasoning
¼ teaspoon dried thyme leaves

> Makes 2 main dishes
> 6 servings each

In 5-qt. casserole combine beans, water and salt; cover. Microwave at High 8 to 12 minutes, or until boiling, stirring once. Let stand, covered, 1 hour.

In 1½- to 2-qt. casserole combine pork cubes, ½ cup onion and the garlic powder; cover. Reduce power to 50% (Medium). Microwave 4 to 6 minutes, or until pork is no longer pink, stirring every 2 minutes. Remove pork and set aside.

In same casserole mix tomatoes, wine, parsley flakes and pepper; cover. Microwave at High 10 minutes, stirring after half the time to break apart tomatoes. Uncover. Microwave 4 to 7 minutes, or until thickened and flavors blend, stirring after half the cooking time. Return pork to casserole; refrigerate.

After beans have stood 1 hour, mix in reserved ½ cup onion and remaining ingredients except refrigerated tomato sauce. Cover. Microwave at 50% (Medium) 1¼ to 1½ hours, or until beans are tender but not soft, stirring 2 or 3 times. Spoon bean mixture into two freezer containers. Top each with half of the tomato mixture. Label and freeze no longer than 2 months.

To serve, remove from one container and place in 2-qt. casserole. Microwave at 70% (Medium-High) 19 to 25 minutes, or until hot, gently breaking apart with fork and stirring 3 or 4 times to mix in tomato sauce. Let stand, covered, 5 minutes.

Wild Rice & Sausage Casserole

3 lbs. bulk seasoned pork
    sausage
4 cups sliced fresh
    mushrooms
⅔ cup chopped celery
1 tablespoon butter or
    margarine
3 cups cooked wild rice,
    page 127
2 cups cooked brown rice,
    page 126
1 can (10¾ oz.) condensed
    cream of mushroom soup
½ cup hot water
¼ cup snipped fresh parsley
½ teaspoon instant chicken
    bouillon granules
½ teaspoon dried marjoram
    leaves
¼ teaspoon dried thyme leaves

Makes 2 main dishes
4 to 6 servings each

Crumble sausage into 3-qt. casserole. Microwave at High 11 to 15 minutes, or until no longer pink, stirring to break apart 2 or 3 times during cooking. Drain and set aside.

In 5-qt. casserole combine mushrooms, celery and butter; cover. Microwave at High 5 to 8 minutes, or until celery is tender-crisp. Drain. Stir in sausage and remaining ingredients. Spoon into two freezer containers. Label and freeze no longer than 1 month.

To serve, remove from one container and place in 1-qt. casserole; cover. Microwave at High 13 to 17 minutes, or until heated, breaking apart as soon as possible, then stirring 2 or 3 times during cooking.

Sausage Loaf

1 medium tomato, finely
  chopped
¼ cup finely chopped onion
¼ cup finely chopped celery
1 lb. bulk mild Italian sausage
½ lb. ground beef
2 eggs, slightly beaten
¾ cup dry seasoned bread
  crumbs
¼ teaspoon ground sage
1 cup shredded or ground fully
  cooked ham

Serves 6 to 8

In 2-qt. casserole combine
tomato, onion and celery; cover.
Microwave at High 3 to 6
minutes, or until tender-crisp,
stirring 1 or 2 times. Mix in
remaining ingredients except
ham. Spread half in foil-lined
9 × 5-in. loaf dish. Spread ham
over top to within ½ inch of
edge. Spread with remaining
sausage mixture. Press to seal
loaf. Freeze until firm. Remove
with foil from loaf dish. Wrap,
label and freeze no longer than
2 months.

To serve, unwrap and place on
roasting rack. Cover with wax
paper. Microwave at High 5
minutes. Rotate rack and
reduce power to 70% (Medium-
High). Microwave 10 minutes,
rotating 1 or 2 times. Shield top
edges with 1-in. wide strips of
foil. Microwave at 70% (Medium-
High) 25 to 30 minutes, or until
internal temperature reaches
160°F. in center, rotating rack
every 4 minutes. Let stand,
covered, 10 minutes.

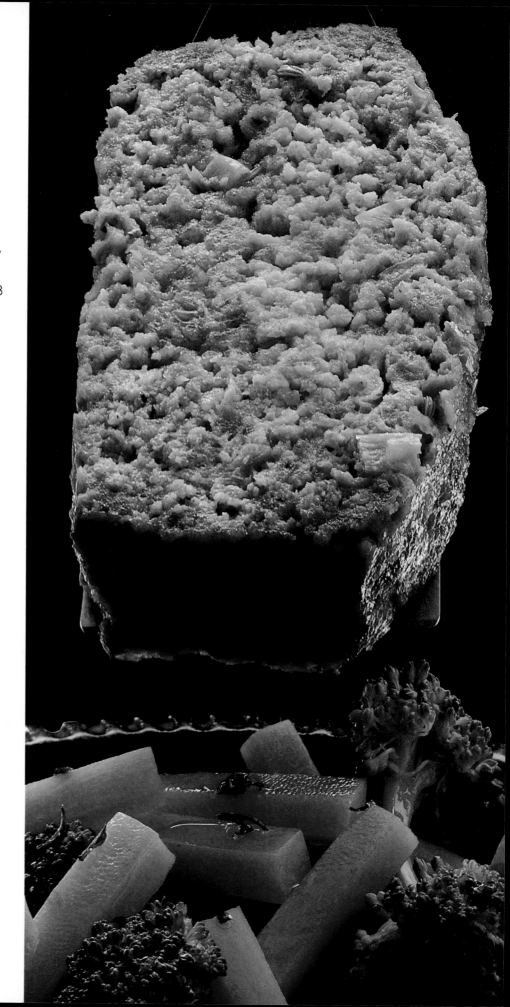

Poultry

Many types of poultry, such as whole turkey, turkey parts, Cornish hens and duckling can be purchased frozen and stored in the freezer. Generally chicken is purchased fresh. Utilize the freezer to stock up on sale-priced poultry. Re-wrap and freeze fresh chicken for future microwaving or cook main dishes and freeze.

Packaging Poultry

Most of the poultry you package for the freezer will probably be chicken. Turkeys, turkey parts, ducklings and Cornish hens are usually frozen when purchased. If you buy them fresh, follow the directions for freezing chickens.

For the microwave-freezer team, plump broiler-fryers are your best choice. Whole chickens are often more economical than chicken pieces. **Do not stuff whole poultry before freezing.**

If you're going to cook chicken in quarters or pieces, take the time to cut it up before freezing. Chicken pieces are easier to wrap airtight and take less freezer space.

How to Package Whole Chickens in Freezer Bags

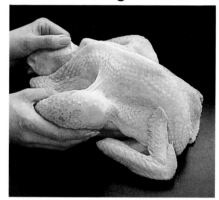

Remove giblets and neck. Rinse chicken inside and out under cold running water; dry.

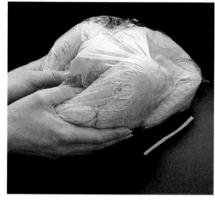

Place chicken in freezer bag, neck end down. Press plastic firmly against chicken to force out air. Or, use water to remove air as directed in next photo.

Lower bag into water, keeping open end above water. Press bag against chicken to force out air bubbles.

Twist bag opening; fold over once. Seal bags with twist tie. Label and freeze no longer than 8 months.

Package giblets and neck separately. Place in small plastic container or freezer bags. Freeze livers, hearts, gizzards and necks separately, if desired. Label and freeze no longer than 3 months. Use in dressings, soups, rumaki or pâté.

How to Package Whole Chickens in Freezer Paper or Foil

Package giblets and neck as directed, opposite. Rinse chicken inside and out under cold running water; dry.

Wrap chicken in plastic wrap, pressing legs and wings close to body and forcing out air.

Overwrap with heavy-duty foil or freezer paper. Label and freeze no longer than 8 months.

How to Package Chicken Pieces in Freezer Paper or Foil

Rinse pieces under cold running water; dry. Divide into meal or recipe-size amounts.

Arrange pieces close together on plastic wrap or freezer paper. Wrap airtight. Overwrap plastic with heavy-duty foil. Label and freeze no longer than 8 months.

How to Package Chicken Pieces in Bags

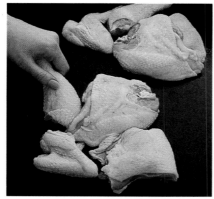

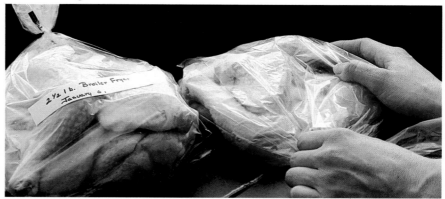

Rinse pieces under cold running water; dry. Divide into meal or recipe-size amounts.

Place chicken pieces close together in freezer bag or heat-sealable pouches. Press out air. Seal bag with twist tie or heat-seal. Label and freeze no longer than 8 months.

Defrosting Poultry

Defrosting is one of the major advantages of a microwave oven. Less flavor and fewer juices are lost when poultry is defrosted just before using it.

Start microwaving when standing time is completed. Poultry pieces defrost quickly. They should be placed on a rack to prevent runaway

cooking. Metal wire, sometimes used to hold the legs of frozen turkeys, can be left in place during defrosting but should be removed during microwaving.

How to Defrost Whole Turkey

Remove wrapping. Place turkey, breast side down, in baking dish. Estimate total defrost time as directed in chart, page 91. Defrost for one-fourth total time.

Check for areas which feel warm. Shield with foil if necessary. Turn turkey breast side up. Defrost for second one-fourth total time.

Shield leg and wing tips and any warm or brown areas with foil. Turn turkey breast side down and rotate dish. Continue defrosting for additional one-fourth total time.

Turn turkey over; defrost remaining time. Remove shields. Spread legs and wings from body; loosen giblets.

Let stand in cool water 20 to 30 minutes, or until giblets and neck can be removed.

Check breast area under wings to be sure it is defrosted. Cavity should be cool but not icy.

How to Defrost Whole Chicken, Duckling & Cornish Hens

Remove wrapping. Place bird on roasting rack, breast side down. Cover with wax paper.

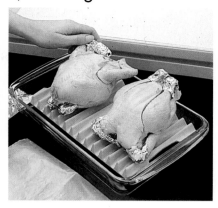

Defrost for half the time, as directed in chart, page 91. Shield leg tips and warm spots.

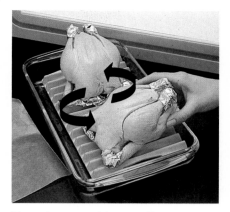

Turn breast side up. Rearrange Cornish hens so sides toward outside are in the center.

Defrost remaining time. Spread legs and wings from body; loosen and remove giblets and neck, if possible.

Place duckling in cool water 5 to 10 minutes, or until giblets and neck can be removed and cavity is cool but not icy.

Let chickens and Cornish hens stand 5 minutes. Remove neck and giblets. Rinse cavity under cold running water. Let stand 10 minutes.

How to Defrost Turkey Breast & Half Turkey

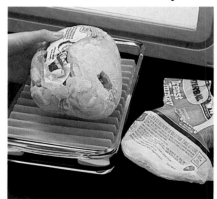

Remove wrapping. Place turkey, breast side down, on roasting rack. Remove gravy packet. Defrost for half the time, as directed in chart, page 91.

Shield warm or brown areas with foil. Turn breast side up. Defrost remaining time; rinse under cold running water.

Let stand 5 to 10 mintutes, or until breast is fully defrosted but still cold.

How to Defrost Turkey Hind Quarters & Legs

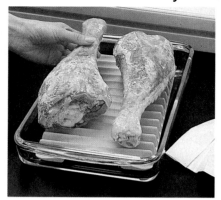

Unwrap pieces; place on roasting rack with meatiest portions to outside. Defrost for half the time as directed in chart, opposite.

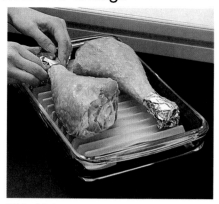

Shield leg tips and warm areas. Separate pieces and turn over. Defrost remaining time, or until surface is pliable but still cool.

Rinse under cold running water. Let stand 5 to 10 minutes, or until thickest part can be pierced to the bone with a skewer.

How to Defrost Chicken Quarters & Pieces

Unwrap; place on roasting rack. Defrost for half the time, as directed in chart, opposite.

Separate pieces. Arrange on rack with meatiest parts to outside of rack. Defrost remaining time.

Let stand 5 to 10 minutes, or until pliable but still cold. Rinse under cold running water.

How to Defrost Boneless Chicken Breasts

Unwrap breasts. Place on roasting rack. Defrost for half the time, as directed in chart, opposite.

Separate breasts. Arrange on rack with least defrosted parts to outside of rack.

Defrost for remaining time, or until chicken is pliable but still very cold. Let stand 5 minutes.

Poultry Defrosting Chart

Type	Defrost Time at 50% (Medium)	Procedure
Turkey		
Whole	3 - 6 min./lb.	Follow photo directions, page 88.
Turkey Breast, Half Turkey	3 - 6 min./lb.	Follow photo directions, page 89.
Turkey Hind Quarters & Legs	3 - 6 min./lb.	Follow photo directions, page 90.
Chicken		
Whole	3 - 5½ min./lb.	Follow photo directions, page 89.
Chicken Quarters & Pieces	3½ - 5½ min./lb.	Follow photo directions, page 90.
Boneless Chicken Breasts	5½ - 8 min./lb.	Follow photo directions, page 90.
Duckling	4½ - 6 min./lb.	Follow photo directions, page 89.
Cornish Hens	5 - 7 min./lb.	Follow photo directions, page 89.

Convenience Poultry Defrosting Chart

Type	Amount	Microwave Time at High	Procedure
Turkey Roast	2 lbs.	High: 5 min., then 50% (Med.): 15 - 35 min.	Set aside gravy packet. Transfer roast from foil pan to 9 × 5-in. loaf dish. Cover with wax paper. Microwave at High. Rotate ¼ turn. Reduce power. Microwave until internal temperature reaches 175°F., rotating 2 or 3 times. Let stand 5 minutes. If preparing gravy, remove roast from dish. Reduce water by ¼ cup. Add gravy mix and water to drippings. Microwave at High 6 to 8 minutes, or until thickened, stirring every 2 minutes.
Precooked Fried Chicken	2 to 3 pieces	2½ - 5 min.	Separate and arrange on roasting rack with meatiest portions to outside of dish. Cover with paper towel. Rearrange, but do not turn over, after half the time. Let stand 2 to 3 minutes on paper towel-lined plate covered with paper towel. Microwave 60-oz. package one-half box at a time.
	4 pieces	4 - 6½ min.	
	16 oz. (5 to 7 pieces)	9 - 11 min.	
	32 oz. (9 to 11 pieces)	15 - 17 min.	
	60 oz. (½ box)	15 - 17 min.	

◄ Paella

1 medium green pepper,
  chopped
1 medium onion, chopped
1 clove garlic, minced
3 tablespoons olive oil
1 can (16 oz.) whole tomatoes,
  cut up
1 can (10¾ oz.) chicken broth
1 cup cubed fully cooked
  ham, ½-in. cubes
½ teaspoon paprika
1 small bay leaf
⅛ teaspoon ground saffron

⅛ teaspoon red pepper sauce
2½ to 3-lb. broiler-fryer chicken,
  cut up
½ lb. raw medium shrimp,
  peeled and deveined
1 can (8 oz.) whole oysters,
  drained, optional

To serve:
1 container frozen White Rice,
  defrosted, page 126
1 cup frozen peas

Makes 2 main dishes
4 to 6 servings each

In 5-qt. casserole combine green pepper, onion, garlic and olive oil; cover. Microwave at High 4 to 7 minutes, or until tender-crisp, stirring 1 or 2 times. Stir in tomatoes, broth, ham, paprika, bay leaf, saffron and red pepper sauce. Add chicken. Re-cover.

Microwave at High 22 to 26 minutes, or until chicken near bone is no longer pink and juices run clear, rearranging and turning pieces over after half the cooking time. Stir in shrimp and oysters. Let stand, covered, 5 minutes. Skim fat; discard. Spoon into two freezer containers. Label and freeze no longer than 4 months.

To serve, defrost rice as directed. Set aside. Remove Paella from one container and place in 2-qt. casserole; cover. Microwave at High 10 minutes. Separate chicken pieces. Stir in rice and peas. Re-cover. Microwave at 70% (Medium-High) 10 to 16 minutes, or until heated, stirring 1 or 2 times. Let stand 5 to 10 minutes.

◄ Chicken With Sour Cream Sauce

2½ to 3-lb. broiler-fryer chicken,
  cut up, skin removed
2 medium carrots, thinly
  sliced
½ cup thinly sliced celery
¼ cup chopped onion
½ teaspoon salt
¼ teaspoon pepper

¼ teaspoon dried thyme
  leaves
1 can (10¾ oz.) condensed
  cream of chicken soup
½ cup water

To serve:
½ cup dairy sour cream

Serves 4 to 6

In 3-qt. casserole place chicken, carrots, celery, onion, salt, pepper and thyme. In small bowl mix soup and water. Pour over chicken and vegetables. Cover. Microwave at High 23 to 30 minutes, or until chicken near bone is no longer pink and juices run clear, rearranging and turning chicken over 2 times. Package in freezer container. Label and freeze no longer than 6 months.

To serve, remove from container and place in 3-qt. casserole. Cover. Microwave at High 5 minutes. Reduce power to 70% (Medium-High). Microwave 20 to 25 minutes, or until heated, breaking up and rearranging pieces 3 or 4 times. Remove chicken. Blend sour cream into sauce. Spoon over chicken. Serve with noodles, if desired.

Lemon-Herb Chicken

¼ cup fresh lemon juice
2 tablespoons dried parsley
  flakes
2 teaspoons dried tarragon
  leaves
1½ teaspoons lemon pepper
1 teaspoon salt
½ teaspoon garlic powder
2½ to 3-lb. broiler-fryer chicken,
  cut up

To serve:

4 thin lemon slices, cut in half
½ cup water
¼ cup fresh lemon juice
1 tablespoon cornstarch
2 teaspoons snipped fresh
  parsley
1½ teaspoons sugar
⅛ teaspoon dried basil leaves
  Dash salt
1 tablespoon butter or
  margarine

Serves 4 to 6

In small bowl mix lemon juice, parsley flakes, tarragon, lemon pepper, salt and garlic powder. If desired, remove skin from chicken. Rub herb mixture evenly onto chicken. Place on wax paper-lined tray. Freeze until firm. Wrap, label and freeze no longer than 4 months.

To serve, unwrap and place in 12 × 8-in. baking dish. Cover with wax paper. Microwave at High 25 to 32 minutes, or until chicken near bone is no longer pink and juices run clear, rearranging 3 or 4 times. Place lemon slices on chicken and let stand while preparing lemon sauce. Blend remaining ingredients except butter in small bowl. Microwave at High 3 to 6 minutes, or until thickened, stirring 2 or 3 times. Stir in butter until melted. Serve sauce over chicken.

Creamy Chicken & Artichokes

Broth:

3 to 3½-lb. broiler-fryer
    chicken, cut up
1 lemon
1 lime
2 cups hot water
1 medium onion, cut into
    8 pieces
1 teaspoon instant chicken
    bouillon granules
¼ teaspoon whole peppercorns
¼ teaspoon dried tarragon
    leaves

To serve:

4 frozen patty shells
1 tablespoon butter or
    margarine
¼ cup sliced almonds
1 pkg. (9 oz.) frozen artichoke
    hearts
¼ cup all-purpose flour
½ cup half and half
2 tablespoons chopped
    pimiento
½ teaspoon sugar
¼ teaspoon salt
¼ teaspoon paprika

Makes 2 main dishes
2 to 4 servings each

How to Microwave Creamy Chicken & Artichokes

Arrange chicken in 5-qt. casserole with meatiest portions to outside. Cut four slices each from the lemon and lime; arrange on top of chicken. Squeeze about 1 tablespoon juice from each remaining half. Sprinkle over chicken.

Add remaining broth ingredients. Cover. Microwave at High 20 to 30 minutes, or until meat near bone is no longer pink and juices run clear, turning over and rearranging pieces every 10 minutes.

Remove chicken from broth; cool. Skim fat; discard. Strain broth. Remove chicken from skin and bones; cut into small pieces. Return to broth. Discard skin and bones. Spoon into two freezer containers. Label and freeze no longer than 4 months.

Coq Au Vin

1 medium onion, thinly sliced and separated into rings
1 clove garlic, minced
4 slices bacon, cut into 1-in. pieces
¼ cup all-purpose flour
¾ cup hot water
¼ cup white wine
2½ to 3½-lb. broiler-fryer chicken, cut up, skin removed
2 cups sliced fresh mushrooms
2 teaspoons dried parsley flakes
½ teaspoon salt
¼ teaspoon dried tarragon leaves
⅛ teaspoon pepper
1 small bay leaf

To serve:
¼ cup white wine

Serves 4 to 6

In small bowl combine onion and garlic; cover. Microwave at High 1½ to 3 minutes, or until tender-crisp. Set aside.

Place bacon in 3-qt. casserole. Microwave at High 4 to 6 minutes, or until crisp, stirring 1 or 2 times. Drain, reserving 1 tablespoon fat in casserole. Crumble bacon and set aside. Mix flour into casserole. Stir in water and ¼ cup wine.

Mix in remaining ingredients except wine for serving; cover. Microwave at High 20 to 25 minutes, or until chicken near bone is no longer pink and juices run clear, turning over and rearranging chicken once and stirring sauce 2 or 3 times. Package in freezer container. Label and freeze no longer than 4 months.

To serve, remove from container and place in 3-qt. casserole. Cover. Microwave at High 10 minutes. Reduce power to 70% (Medium-High). Microwave 20 to 26 minutes, or until heated, breaking apart and rearranging 2 or 3 times. Stir in ¼ cup wine.

To serve, prepare four patty shells as directed on package. Set aside. Remove broth and chicken from one container and place in 2-qt. casserole; cover. Microwave at 70% (Medium-High) 8 to 9 minutes, stirring to break apart 2 times. Set aside.

Melt butter in medium bowl at High 30 to 45 seconds. Add almonds, tossing to coat. Microwave at High 3½ to 4½ minutes, or until light brown, stirring every minute. Drain on paper towels. Place artichoke hearts in 1-qt. casserole; cover. Microwave at High 5 to 6 minutes, or until heated, stirring once to break apart. Drain.

Remove ½ cup broth. Blend with flour. Return to broth. Stir in half and half, pimiento, sugar, salt and paprika. Microwave, uncovered, at 50% (Medium) 8 to 9 minutes, or until thickened, stirring every 2 minutes. Add artichokes and toasted almonds. Spoon into patty shells to serve.

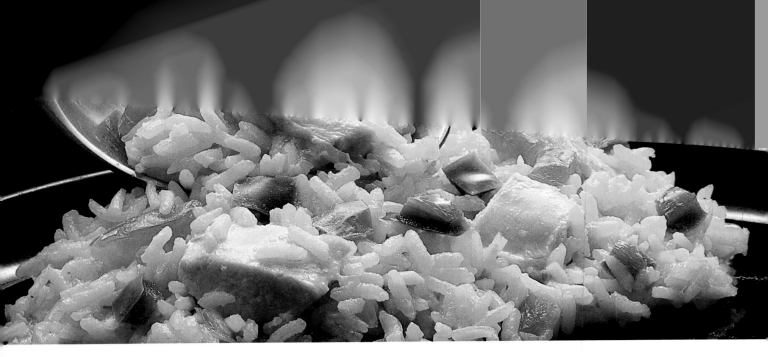

Stewed Chicken

2½ to 3-lb. broiler-fryer chicken, cut up
4 cups hot water
1 stalk celery, cut into 4 pieces
1 small onion, cut into 4 pieces
1 small carrot, cut into 4 pieces
1 teaspoon salt
¼ teaspoon pepper

Makes 7 to 8 cups

In 5-qt. casserole combine all ingredients; cover. Microwave at High 25 to 32 minutes, or until chicken near bone is no longer pink and juices run clear, rearranging 2 or 3 times. Remove chicken from broth. Remove chicken from skin and bones; cut into bite-sized pieces. Return to broth. Discard skin and bones. Skim fat from broth. Remove vegetables with slotted spoon; discard.

Spoon chicken and broth into freezer container. Label and freeze no longer than 6 months.

To defrost, remove from container and place in 2-qt. casserole. Microwave at High 22 to 28 minutes, or until warm, breaking apart and stirring 3 or 4 times.

Chicken & Yellow Rice ▲

1 container frozen Stewed Chicken, defrosted, left
1 medium onion, chopped
1 medium green pepper, chopped
1 clove garlic, minced
3 tablespoons olive oil
2¼ cups uncooked long grain rice
1 medium tomato, chopped
1½ teaspoons salt
¼ teaspoon ground saffron
⅛ teaspoon pepper
1 bay leaf

Serves 4 to 6

Measure 4 cups broth from stewed chicken; set aside. Refrigerate any additional broth for use in other recipes. In 5-qt. casserole combine onion, green pepper, garlic and olive oil; cover. Microwave at High 4 to 6 minutes, or until tender.

Mix in broth and remaining ingredients except chicken; cover. Microwave at High 10 minutes. Reduce power to 50% (Medium). Microwave 26 to 33 minutes, or until rice is tender. Stir in chicken. Let stand, covered, 5 minutes.

Chicken & Wheat Dumplings

1 cup buttermilk baking mix
½ cup whole wheat flour
⅓ cup milk
1 container frozen Stewed Chicken, defrosted, left

Serves 4 to 6

Blend baking mix, flour and milk. Microwave stewed chicken at High 5 minutes. Drop dumplings by heaping tablespoons onto hot broth. Cover.

Microwave at High 3 minutes. Uncover. Microwave at High 5 to 8 minutes, or until dumplings are set and broth is thickened, gently turning dumplings over and rearranging once.

Rice-Stuffed Chicken Breast ►

2 whole boneless chicken
   breasts, split and skin
   removed
½ cup chopped fresh
   mushrooms
2 tablespoons butter or
   margarine
2 tablespoons pine nuts
1 tablespoon chopped green
   onion
1 tablespoon snipped fresh
   parsley
⅛ teaspoon dried rosemary
   leaves
   Dash dried tarragon leaves
   Dash pepper
¾ cup cooked rice*
1 egg, beaten
1 tablespoon milk
⅓ cup dry seasoned bread
   crumbs

Serves 4

Pound chicken breasts to ¼-in. thickness. In small bowl combine mushrooms, butter, pine nuts, onion, parsley, rosemary, tarragon and pepper. Cover. Microwave at High 1½ to 2 minutes, or until butter melts. Stir in rice.

Place about ¼ cup of stuffing near one end of each chicken breast. Roll up, folding in sides. In small bowl combine egg and milk. Brush chicken breasts with egg mixture, then gently roll in bread crumbs. Freeze seam side down on wax paper-lined tray until firm. Wrap individually. Label and freeze no longer than 6 months.

To serve, unwrap four chicken breasts; arrange on roasting rack. Microwave at High 5 minutes. Rearrange. Reduce power to 50% (Medium). Microwave 11 to 17 minutes, or until chicken is no longer pink and stuffing is hot, rearranging 3 or 4 times.

*For extra flavor, substitute chicken broth for water when preparing rice.

Stuffed Chicken Breast a L'Orange pictured on page 84

2 whole boneless chicken
   breasts, split and skin
   removed

Stuffing:
2 tablespoons dry vermouth
2 tablespoons raisins
¼ cup finely chopped celery
3 tablespoons butter or
   margarine
2 tablespoons chopped green
   onion
½ cup dry bread crumbs
1½ teaspoons grated orange
   peel

⅛ teaspoon garlic powder

To serve:
¼ cup orange juice
¼ cup water
1½ teaspoons cornstarch
2 tablespoons raisins
1½ teaspoons packed brown
   sugar
⅛ teaspoon ground allspice
⅛ teaspoon salt
   Dash ground ginger
   Dash pepper
4 thin orange slices

Serves 4

Pound chicken breasts to ¼-in. thickness. Microwave vermouth at High 20 to 30 seconds, or until warm. Stir in raisins.

In 1-qt. casserole combine celery, butter and green onion. Cover. Microwave at High 1½ to 3 minutes, or until vegetables are tender-crisp, stirring 1 or 2 times. Stir in bread crumbs, orange peel, garlic powder and raisin mixture. Set aside.

Place about ¼ cup stuffing near one end of each chicken breast. Roll up, folding in sides. Secure with two wooden picks. Freeze on wax paper-lined tray until firm. Wrap individually. Label and freeze no longer than 6 months.

To serve, unwrap four chicken breasts and arrange in 8 × 8-in. baking dish. Cover with wax paper. Microwave at High 5 minutes. Rearrange. Reduce power to 50% (Medium). Microwave 10 to 18 minutes, or until chicken is no longer pink and juices run clear, rearranging 1 or 2 times. Let stand, covered. In small bowl mix orange juice, water and cornstarch. Stir in remaining ingredients except orange slices. Microwave at High 2 to 3½ minutes, or until thickened, stirring 1 or 2 times. Spoon glaze over chicken breasts, placing one orange slice on each.

◀ Gingered Chicken & Pea Pods

2 whole boneless chicken breasts, skin removed, cut into 3 × ½-in. strips

Marinade:

3 tablespoons water
1 tablespoon sherry
2 teaspoons soy sauce
1½ teaspoons honey
⅛ teaspoon dry mustard
⅛ teaspoon ground ginger
⅛ teaspoon instant minced garlic
⅛ teaspoon onion powder
1 thin lemon slice

To serve:

1 pkg. (6 oz.) frozen pea pods
¼ cup water
2 tablespoons oyster sauce
2 teaspoons cornstarch
1 teaspoon instant chicken bouillon granules
1 cup sliced fresh mushrooms
3 tablespoons chopped green onion

Serves 4 to 6

Place chicken strips in freezer container. In 2-cup measure combine all marinade ingredients. Microwave at High 1 to 2 minutes, or until boiling and honey dissolves, stirring once. Remove lemon slice. Pour over chicken strips. Refrigerate 2 hours. Label and freeze no longer than 3 months.

To serve, place pea pods package in oven. Microwave at High 1 to 2 minutes, or until defrosted and pea pods separate. Set aside. Remove chicken strips from container and place in 1½-qt. casserole; cover. Microwave at High 4 to 8 minutes, or until chicken can be broken apart.

In 1-cup measure mix water, oyster sauce, cornstarch and bouillon granules. Stir into chicken and marinade in casserole. Add mushrooms and green onion; cover. Microwave at High 5 to 9 minutes, or until chicken is no longer pink, stirring 2 or 3 times. Stir in pea pods. Let stand, covered, 5 minutes.

Tomato-Mushroom Chicken ▶

1 cup sliced fresh mushrooms
1 medium onion, thinly sliced
2 tablespoons olive oil
1 clove garlic, minced
1 can (16 oz.) whole tomatoes
1 can (6 oz.) tomato paste
¼ cup dry white wine

1 small bay leaf
1 teaspoon dried basil leaves
½ teaspoon salt
¼ teaspoon pepper
3 whole boneless chicken breasts, skin removed, cut into 1½-in. pieces

Serves 4 to 6

In 3-qt. casserole combine mushrooms, onion, olive oil and garlic; cover. Microwave at High 5 to 8 minutes, or until onion is tender, stirring once. Stir in remaining ingredients; cover. Microwave at High 10 to 15 minutes, or until chicken is no longer pink, stirring 2 or 3 times. Spoon into freezer container. Label and freeze no longer than 6 months.

To serve, remove from container and place in 2-qt. casserole; cover. Microwave at High 18 to 21 minutes, or until hot, breaking apart with fork and stirring 2 or 3 times. Serve over rice or spinach noodles, if desired.

Stuffed Fruit-Glazed Chicken Thighs

1 medium apple, cored and
    chopped
1 medium orange, sectioned
    and chopped
½ cup uncooked instant rice
2 tablespoons chopped dried
    chives
¼ cup orange marmalade,
    divided
1 tablespoon plus 2 teaspoons
    butter or margarine, divided
¼ teaspoon ground coriander
⅛ teaspoon salt
⅛ teaspoon pepper
8 chicken thighs
¼ teaspoon bouquet sauce
1 teaspoon sesame seed

                    Serves 4 to 6

In medium bowl combine apple, orange, rice, chives, 1 table-spoon marmalade, 1 tablespoon butter, the coriander, salt and pepper. Cover with plastic wrap. Microwave at High 2 to 4 minutes, or until very hot, stirring after half the time. Let stand, covered, 5 minutes.

Loosen skin from chicken to form a pocket. Stuff each pocket with 2 heaping tablespoons mixture. Arrange stuffed thighs on roasting rack. Set aside.

In 2-cup measure combine remaining 3 tablespoons marmalade, 2 teaspoons butter and the bouquet sauce. Microwave at High 30 to 45 seconds, or until heated, stirring after half the time. Brush over stuffed thighs. Sprinkle with sesame seed. Microwave at High 12 to 15 minutes, or until chicken near bone is no longer pink, rotating and rearranging 2 times. Wrap, label and freeze no longer than 1 month.

To serve, unwrap and place in 8 × 8-in. baking dish. Microwave at 50% (Medium) 20 to 30 minutes, or until heated, rotating and rearranging 2 times.

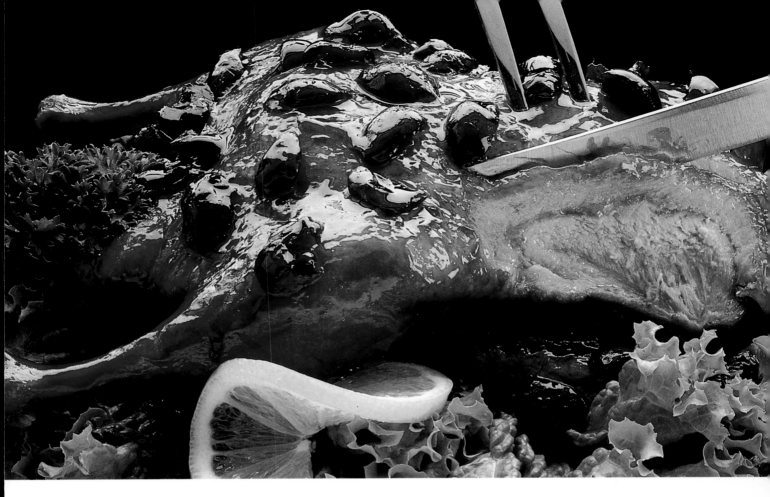

Duckling With Cherry Glaze ▲

Glaze:
1 can (16 oz.) dark sweet
  pitted cherries, coarsely
  chopped, ⅓ cup juice
  reserved
2 teaspoons cornstarch
2 tablespoons red wine or
  water
2 tablespoons honey

¼ teaspoon dry mustard
  Dash ground ginger

Duckling:
4½ to 5½-lb. frozen duckling
  1 stalk celery, cut into 4
    pieces
  1 small onion, cut into 4
    pieces

Serves 4

In 1-qt. measure combine reserved cherry juice and cornstarch.
Blend in remaining glaze ingredients except cherries. Microwave at
High 1 to 2½ minutes, or until thickened, stirring with fork 1 or 2
times until smooth. Stir in cherries; set aside.

Unwrap frozen duckling and place on roasting rack, breast side
down. Microwave at High 10 minutes. Remove giblets. Stuff cavity
with celery and onion. Turn duckling breast side up. Estimate
remaining cooking time at 12 to 16 minutes per pound. Microwave
at 50% (Medium), or until legs move easily and juices run clear,
glazing, turning over and draining fat 2 or 3 times. Use one-third of
glaze each time. Shield wings and tail with foil during cooking, if
necessary. Spoon any remaining glaze over duckling. Let stand,
tented with foil, 5 minutes.

Turkey Breast

2½ to 3½-lb. frozen turkey
  breast

Serves 4 to 6

Unwrap turkey breast and place
on roasting rack, skin side up.
Cover with wax paper. Estimate
total cooking time at 17 to 22
minutes per pound. If turkey
contains a gravy package,
remove package after the first
10 to 15 minutes of cooking
time. Microwave at 50%
(Medium), or until juices run
clear and internal temperature
at meatiest part reaches 170°F.,
rotating rack and turning breast
over 2 times. Shield, if
necessary. Remove wax paper
during last half of cooking time.
Baste with butter during cooking, if desired. Let stand, tented
with foil, 10 to 20 minutes.
Glaze with jelly, if desired.

Fish & Seafood

The microwave-freezer team is especially useful for the fisherman, but you can also put it to creative use if your "catch" comes from the supermarket.

Defrost and prepare frozen fish quickly in the microwave. Or, prepare fresh fish and freeze to be quickly defrosted and reheated in the microwave at a later time.

Salmon Steaks With Sesame-Dill Sauce

Sauce:
¼ cup butter or margarine
¼ cup fresh lemon juice
 1 tablespoon sesame seed
½ teaspoon sugar
¼ teaspoon dried dill weed
¼ teaspoon salt
⅛ teaspoon garlic powder

 4 frozen salmon steaks, 1-in. thick (about 2 lbs.), defrosted, page 105

Serves 4

In 2-cup measure combine sauce ingredients. Microwave at High 1 to 2 minutes, or until mixture is hot and butter melts, stirring once during cooking.

Place salmon steaks on roasting rack. Brush with sauce. Cover with wax paper. Microwave at 50% (Medium) 10 minutes. Turn steaks over. Brush with sauce; re-cover. Microwave at 50% (Medium) 8 to 16 minutes, or until fish flakes easily with fork. Let stand 3 to 5 minutes. Serve with remaining sauce.

Freezing & Defrosting Fish

If you are lucky enough to know a fisherman or live close to a fresh-fish market, take advantage of seasonal supply and store fish in your freezer. Check with your fish market to make sure the fish was never frozen. Do not refreeze fish because it lowers the quality. To preserve quality, freeze fish as soon as possible after catching.

Keep fresh fish well chilled until you're ready to pan dress or fillet them. Freeze prepared fish in meal-size packages and be sure to wrap them airtight to avoid freezer burn. Label with type of fish, weight or number of pieces and date.

How to Prepare Fish for Freezing

Scale, gut or fillet fish, as desired. Wipe fresh fish with paper towel.

Cut large fish into ¾-in. steaks, serving-size fillets or leave fish whole for stuffing. Wipe again with paper towel, if desired.

How to Freeze Fish in Water

Select a container slightly larger than fish. A loaf pan lined with foil or a shallow plastic dish works well.

Place fish in dish. Add just enough cold water to cover. The amount of water affects defrosting time.

Freeze until firm. Remove from container; wrap airtight. Label and freeze no longer than 6 months.

How to Freeze Fish Without Water

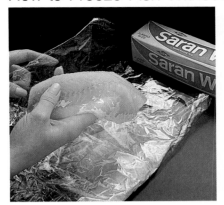

Separate fish with double thickness of plastic wrap or freezer paper.

Wrap fish in plastic wrap or place in plastic bag, pressing out air.

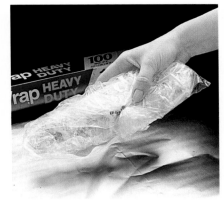

Overwrap with heavy-duty foil or freezer paper. Label and freeze no longer than 4 months.

How to Defrost Fish Frozen in Water   50% (Medium)   8 - 13 min./lb.

Hold fish under cold running water to loosen packaging, if necessary. Remove. Place fish in 12 × 8-in. baking dish. Cover with wax paper.

Defrost until fish is pliable but still icy in center or thick areas, removing when defrosted. Drain water 1 or 2 times, or use roasting rack. Let stand 10 to 15 minutes to complete defrosting. Pat dry.

How to Defrost Fish Frozen Without Water   50% (Medium)   3 - 5 min./lb.

Open package, removing any foil. If pieces can be separated, place them in dish in which they will be cooked. Place dish or package in oven.

Defrost for half the time. Separate, rearrange or turn fish over, bringing less defrosted parts to top and outside of dish.

Defrost remaining time, or until fish is pliable on outside but icy in center or thick areas. Let stand 5 minutes. Pat dry.

Scallop-Salmon Kabobs

2 fresh salmon steaks (1 lb. each)
8 small white onions
1 medium green pepper, cut into 16 pieces
8 wooden skewers, 10-in.
1 lb. fresh scallops, larger scallops cut into 1-in. pieces
1 lemon, cut into 8 wedges
1 tablespoon butter or margarine

To serve:
¼ cup plus 2 tablespoons butter or margarine
¼ cup vermouth
½ teaspoon dried marjoram leaves
Dash pepper

Makes 2 main dishes
4 servings each

How to Microwave Scallop-Salmon Kabobs

Remove bones from salmon; cut into 1-in. cubes. Thread onion and green pepper on each skewer, then alternate three scallops with two salmon cubes. Continue with green pepper and lemon wedge.

Melt butter in custard cup at High 30 to 45 seconds. Lightly brush butter over seafood. Freeze on wax paper-lined tray until firm. Wrap in groups of four. Label and freeze no longer than 2 months.

To serve, place ¼ cup plus 2 tablespoons butter in small bowl. Microwave at High 45 to 60 seconds, or until butter melts. Beat in remaining ingredients with wire whip.

Unwrap one package and place on roasting rack. Cover with wax paper. Reduce power to 50% (Medium).

Microwave 19 to 23 minutes, or until scallops are opaque and flake easily with fork, basting with sauce and rearranging 2 or 3 times. (Stir sauce with wire whip before basting.)

Increase power to High. Microwave remaining sauce 30 to 60 seconds, or until heated. Stir. Serve with kabobs.

Individual Salmon Loaves

1 can (15½ oz.) salmon,
  drained and flaked
2 eggs
½ cup saltine cracker crumbs
¼ cup milk
1 teaspoon dried chopped
  chives
½ teaspoon grated lemon peel
½ teaspoon salt
⅛ teaspoon pepper

To serve:

2 teaspoons butter or
  margarine
2 teaspoons cornstarch
⅔ cup water
1 tablespoon snipped fresh
  parsley
1 teaspoon grated lemon peel
1 teaspoon fresh lemon juice
¼ teaspoon sugar
  Dash dried basil leaves
  Dash pepper

Serves 4

In medium bowl mix salmon, eggs, cracker crumbs, milk, chives, lemon peel, salt and pepper. Press evenly into four 6-oz. foil-lined custard cups. Freeze until firm. Remove with foil from custard cups. Wrap, label and freeze no longer than 1 month.

To serve, unwrap and place in four 6-oz. custard cups. Cover with wax paper. Microwave at 50% (Medium) 15 to 22 minutes, or until set and no longer moist in center, rotating cups 3 or 4 times during cooking. Remove from cups, top side up. Cover and let stand while preparing sauce.

Place butter in 2-cup measure. Microwave at High 30 to 45 seconds, or until butter melts. Stir in cornstarch. Blend in remaining ingredients. Microwave at High 1½ to 2½ minutes, or until thick, stirring every 30 seconds. Pour over individual loaves to serve.

Stuffed Trout

½ cup chopped celery
¼ cup chopped green onion
¼ cup butter or margarine
1 can (2½ oz.) mushroom
    stems and pieces, drained
2 tablespoons snipped fresh
    parsley
1 teaspoon grated lemon peel
¼ teaspoon salt
⅛ teaspoon dried basil leaves
⅛ teaspoon pepper
2 slices white bread, cut into
    ¼-in. cubes
½ lb. raw medium shrimp,
    shelled and deveined,
    page 110
4 fresh drawn* trout
    (about 2 lbs.)

Serves 4

In medium bowl combine
celery, green onion and butter.
Microwave at High 4 to 6
minutes, or until celery is
tender. Stir in mushrooms,
parsley, lemon peel, salt, basil
and pepper. Stir in bread cubes
to coat. Cut shrimp into ¼- to
½-in. pieces; mix into stuffing.

Spoon one-fourth of stuffing into
each trout. Freeze on wax
paper-lined tray until firm. Wrap,
label and freeze no longer than
2 months.

To serve, unwrap and place on
baking sheet or roasting rack.
Cover with wax paper. Microwave at 70% (Medium-High) 23
to 29 minutes, or until fish near
backbone flakes easily with fork
and shrimp are opaque,
rearranging fish 1 or 2 times
during cooking.

*Whole fish, gutted.

Crab-Stuffed Red Snapper

½ cup chopped, seeded,
    peeled tomato
⅓ cup thinly sliced celery
¼ cup chopped green pepper
2 tablespoons chopped onion
1 tablespoon snipped fresh
    parsley
1 cup shredded Monterey Jack
    cheese
1 can (6½ oz.) crab meat,
    drained
2 tablespoons chili sauce
½ teaspoon fresh lemon juice
¼ teaspoon ground coriander
⅛ teaspoon pepper
3 to 3½-lb. fresh dressed*
    red snapper or lake trout

Serves 4 to 6

In 1-qt. casserole combine
tomato, celery, green pepper,
onion and parsley; cover.
Microwave at High 2 to 3½
minutes, or until vegetables are
tender, stirring after half the
time. Drain. Stir in remaining
ingredients except fish. Spoon
crab mixture into fish cavity.
Freeze on wax paper-lined tray
until firm. Wrap, label and
freeze no longer than 3 months.

To serve, unwrap and place on
baking sheet or roasting rack.
Cover with wax paper. Microwave at High 3 minutes. Reduce power to 70% (Medium-
High). Microwave 18 to 23
minutes, or until fish near
backbone flakes easily with fork,
turning over once during cooking and rotating 2 or 3 times.
Let stand 5 to 10 minutes.

*Scaled, gutted, fins, tail and
head removed.

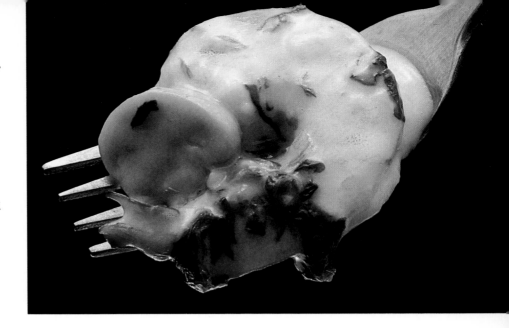

Shrimp Rockefeller ▲

1 can (10¾ oz.) cream of
    mushroom soup
1 cup shredded Cheddar
    cheese
1 can (4 oz.) sliced
    mushrooms, drained
2 tablespoons sherry
1 tablespoon milk
¼ teaspoon salt
    Dash pepper
1 lb. raw medium shrimp,
    shelled and deveined,
    page 110

To serve:
1 tablespoon butter or
    margarine
3 tablespoons dry seasoned
    bread crumbs
2 teaspoons dried parsley
    flakes
¼ teaspoon paprika
2 pkgs. (10 oz. each) frozen
    chopped spinach

Serves 4 to 6

In medium bowl mix soup, cheese, mushrooms, sherry, milk, salt
and pepper. Stir in shrimp. Pour into 1½-qt. foil-lined casserole.
Freeze until firm. Remove with foil from casserole. Wrap, label and
freeze no longer than 2 months.

To serve, place butter in small bowl. Microwave at High 30 to 45
seconds, or until butter melts. Stir in bread crumbs, parsley flakes
and paprika. Set aside.

Place two spinach packages in oven. Microwave at High 5 to 8
minutes, or until warm, rearranging after half the time. Drain,
pressing to remove all liquid. Set aside.

Unwrap shrimp mixture and place in medium bowl. Cover with wax
paper. Microwave at 50% (Medium) 8 to 11 minutes, or until
defrosted, stirring gently with fork to break apart as soon as
possible, then stirring 3 or 4 times more during cooking. (Mixture is
cool and shrimp remains icy.)

Spread spinach in 1½-qt. casserole. Spoon shrimp mixture evenly
over spinach. Cover with wax paper. Microwave at High 3 minutes.
Gently rearrange shrimp; re-cover. Reduce power to 70%
(Medium-High). Microwave 9 to 12 minutes, or until shrimp are
opaque and casserole is heated, gently rearranging shrimp 2 or 3
times during cooking. Sprinkle with seasoned bread crumbs;
cover. Let stand 3 to 5 minutes.

Stuffed Shrimp

1 lb. raw large shrimp in shells
⅓ cup chopped celery
1 tablespoon finely chopped
    onion
2 tablespoons butter or
    margarine
⅔ cup rich round cracker
    crumbs
1 tablespoon chopped
    pimiento, optional
⅛ teaspoon garlic salt
5 or 6 drops red pepper sauce
    or ½ teaspoon grated
    lemon rind, optional

To serve:
2 tablespoons butter or
    margarine

Serves 4 to 6

How to Microwave Stuffed Shrimp

Clean shrimp by loosening shell from the leg side. Peel off carefully, leaving tail intact. Make a cut down middle of back with a knife from tail to thick end.

Do not cut all the way through until the thick end of the shrimp. With point of knife, loosen and remove the vein. To butterfly, flatten the cut thick end.

Combine celery, onion and 2 tablespoons butter in small bowl. Microwave at High 1½ to 2½ minutes, or until tender, stirring once. Stir in cracker crumbs, pimiento, garlic salt and red pepper sauce.

Spoon stuffing on shrimp; press lightly. Freeze on wax paper-lined tray until firm. Package in freezer container with wax paper between layers. Label and freeze no longer than 2 months.

To serve, remove from container and arrange on roasting rack. Cover with wax paper. Microwave at 70% (Medium-High) 8 to 12 minutes, or until shrimp are opaque, rearranging 3 or 4 times.

Let stand 3 to 5 minutes. Place 2 tablespoons butter in 6-oz. custard cup. Microwave at High 30 to 45 seconds, or until butter melts. Drizzle over shrimp.

110

Seafood Casserole

1½ cups thinly sliced celery
2 tablespoons finely chopped onion
2 tablespoons butter or margarine
1 pkg. (10 oz.) frozen peas
1 can (10¾ oz.) cream of chicken soup
1 can (7¾ oz.) salmon, undrained, boned and flaked
1 can (6½ oz.) tuna, undrained
1 jar (2 oz.) chopped pimiento, drained
2¾ cups uncooked instant rice
¾ cup sliced almonds
½ cup mayonnaise or salad dressing
1¼ cups milk
2 hard cooked eggs, finely chopped
½ teaspoon salt
⅛ teaspoon pepper

Makes two main dishes
4 to 6 servings each

In 3-qt. casserole combine celery, onion and butter; cover. Microwave at High 3 to 4 minutes, or until celery is tender-crisp, stirring once. Mix in remaining ingredients. Spoon into two freezer containers. Label and freeze no longer than 2 months.

To serve, remove from one container and place in 1-qt. casserole. Cover. Microwave at 70% (Medium-High) 10 to 15 minutes, or until heated, stirring 2 or 3 times. Sprinkle with sliced almonds, if desired. Cover and let stand 5 minutes.

Fish Almondine ▲

¾ cup finely chopped slivered almonds
½ cup dry seasoned bread crumbs
2 teaspoons snipped fresh parsley
2 teaspoons lemon pepper
1 teaspoon paprika
½ teaspoon salt

1 tablespoon butter or margarine
1 egg
1 lb. fresh fish fillets

Sauce:
¼ cup butter or margarine
⅓ cup slivered almonds
Dash pepper

Serves 4 to 6

In pie plate or on wax paper combine finely chopped almonds, bread crumbs, parsley, lemon pepper, paprika and salt. Set aside.

Place 1 tablespoon butter in pie plate. Microwave at High 30 to 45 seconds, or until butter melts. Blend in egg. Dip fillets in egg mixture, then coat with almond-crumb mixture. Place coated fillets in single layer on wax paper-lined tray; freeze until firm. Wrap, label and freeze no longer than 3 months.

Place ¼ cup butter in pie plate. Microwave at High 45 to 60 seconds, or until butter melts. Stir in slivered almonds and pepper. Microwave at High 2 to 3 minutes, or until light brown, stirring 3 or 4 times during cooking. Spoon into small container. Label and freeze no longer than 3 months.

To serve, remove sauce from container and place in small bowl. Microwave at High 2½ to 4 minutes, or until heated and bubbly, stirring after half the time to break apart. Set aside. Unwrap and arrange fillets on roasting rack or baking sheet. Cover with wax paper. Microwave at 70% (Medium-High) 9 to 13 minutes, or until fish flakes easily with fork, rearranging 3 or 4 times during cooking. Remove wax paper during last 2 minutes of cooking. Let stand 1 to 2 mintues. Serve with sauce.

Skewered Fish & Caper-Butter Sauce

1 lb. fresh fish fillets
¼ cup dry seasoned bread
  crumbs
⅛ teaspoon dried basil leaves
4 wooden skewers, 10-in.

To serve:
½ cup butter or margarine,
  divided
2 tablespoons capers
1 small clove garlic, minced
⅛ teaspoon salt
⅛ teaspoon pepper
  Dash dry mustard

Serves 4

How to Microwave Skewered Fish & Caper-Butter Sauce

Cut fillets lengthwise into 1-in. wide strips. Place bread crumbs and basil in shallow dish or on wax paper. Coat fish strips with crumbs.

Thread one-fourth of strips on each skewer at 3-in. intervals, accordion-style. Place on wax paper-lined tray. Freeze until firm. Wrap, label and freeze no longer than 3 months.

To serve, unwrap and place on roasting rack. Cover with wax paper. Microwave at 70% (Medium-High) 5 to 9 minutes, or until fish flakes easily with fork, rearranging twice.

Cover and let stand while preparing caper-butter sauce. Place 1 tablespoon butter and remaining ingredients in small bowl.

Microwave at High 2 to 3 minutes, or until garlic begins to brown, stirring once. Add remaining 7 tablespoons of butter. Melt at High 45 seconds to 1¼ minutes. Stir.

Place fish on serving plate. Remove the skewers by twisting and pulling out carefully. Spoon caper-butter sauce over fish.

Poached Fish With Cucumber Sauce ▶

¼ cup water
3 slices lemon
3 slices onion
3 whole peppercorns
1 bay leaf
¼ teaspoon salt
1 lb. frozen fish fillets,
    defrosted, page 105

Sauce:

1 tablespoon finely chopped
    onion
½ cup dairy sour cream
½ cup diced seeded cucumber
2 tablespoons milk
1 teaspoon fresh lemon juice
¼ teaspoon salt
⅛ teaspoon ground nutmeg
    Dash pepper

Serves 4 to 6

In 12 × 8-in. baking dish combine water, lemon slices, onion slices, peppercorns, bay leaf and salt. Cover with plastic wrap. Microwave at High 4 minutes. Stir. Arrange fillets in baking dish with thickest portions to the outside. Re-cover. Microwave at High 4 to 7 minutes, or until fish flakes easily with fork, rotating dish ½ turn after half the time. Place fillets on serving plate. Cover and set aside.

Place 1 tablespoon onion in small bowl; cover. Microwave at High 30 to 60 seconds, or until tender. Stir in remaining sauce ingredients. Reduce power to 50% (Medium). Microwave 1½ to 3 minutes, or until heated, stirring every 30 seconds. Serve sauce over fish fillets.

Fillets Creole

½ cup chopped green pepper
½ cup chopped celery
¼ cup chopped green onion
1 clove garlic, minced
2 tablespoons olive oil
1 can (16 oz.) whole
    tomatoes, cut up,
    undrained
1 can (8 oz.) tomato sauce
1 can (6 oz.) tomato paste
¼ cup white wine or water
1 tablespoon lemon juice

1½ teaspoons dried parsley
    flakes
1½ teaspoons sugar
¾ teaspoon salt
¼ teaspoon dried basil leaves
¼ teaspoon dry mustard
⅛ to ¼ teaspoon cayenne
1 bay leaf

To serve:

1 lb. frozen fish fillets,
    defrosted, page 105

Makes 2 main dishes
4 servings each

In 3-qt. casserole combine green pepper, celery, green onion, garlic and olive oil. Microwave at High 4 to 7 minutes, or until tender. Stir in remaining ingredients except fish fillets. Cover.

Microwave at High 5 minutes. Stir. Reduce power to 50% (Medium). Microwave, uncovered, 15 to 18 minutes, or until flavors blend, stirring 2 or 3 times. Cool. Spoon into two freezer containers. Label and freeze no longer than 3 months

To serve, defrost fillets as directed. Remove sauce from one container; place in 1-qt. casserole. Cover. Microwave at High 4 to 7 minutes, or until defrosted, breaking apart and stirring 2 or 3 times.

Arrange fillets in 12 × 8-in. baking dish. Cover with wax paper. Microwave at High 3 minutes, rotating dish once. Spoon sauce over top. Cover with wax paper. Microwave at High 4 to 8 minutes, or until fish flakes easily with fork, rotating dish once.

The microwave oven quickly blanches small batches of vegetables for freezing without heating your kitchen. You can also prepare interesting vegetable recipes when convenient and freeze them for future use.

Blanching & Freezing Vegetables

Blanching inactivates the enzymes which cause vegetables to lose vitamins, flavor and color. Vegetables blanched at the peak of freshness and flavor retain quality and vitamin content.

The microwave oven blanches small amounts of vegetables without creating heat and steam in your kitchen. If you're a gardener, harvest vegetables as they reach the peak of flavor rather than trying to preserve the whole crop at one time.

When you wish to blanch several batches, prepare the second while the first is in the oven. Don't try to increase the quantities done at one time. Cook green vegetables only until color brightens. Other vegetables should remain very crisp. Then, drain and cool immediately in iced water.

Freezing water in plastic ice cream tubs is a convenient way of making ice for cooling the vegetables. Freeze water several days before you plan to use it. Have iced water ready in the sink or large container before microwaving vegetables.

Vegetables can be frozen by the batch in small freezer containers, cartons, or bags. Larger amounts should be loose-packed in reclosable bags, so you can remove the amount needed and return the rest to the freezer.

How to Blanch Vegetables

Clean vegetables thoroughly. Cut into small pieces, if possible. Slices, 1-in. lengths or flowerets freeze and microwave easily and evenly.

Place pieces in casserole with water; cover. Microwave as directed in the chart, or until vegetables are pliable but crisp and color brightens. Drain.

Plunge vegetables immediately into iced water to stop the cooking process. Cool completely. Drain thoroughly.

How to Freeze Blanched Vegetables

Pack small amounts into freezer bags, boxes or pint containers, leaving ½ inch headspace for expansion. Seal.

Loose-pack for large bags or containers by spreading pieces on baking sheet. Freeze, then pack in bags or boxes and seal.

Label with name of vegetable and date. Store no longer than 12 months.

Blanching & Microwaving Vegetable Chart

Type	Amount	Blanching* Time at High	Microwaving* Time at High	Special Microwaving Instructions
Beans				
Green, Wax	2 cups	5 - 6 min.	5 - 7 min.	Use ¼ cup water. Add ¼ teaspoon salt.
Lima	2 cups	3½ - 5 min.	4 - 7 min.	Use ¼ cup water. Add ¼ teaspoon salt.
Broccoli				
Pieces	4 cups	4 - 5½ min.	2 cups: 5 - 7 min.	Use 2-qt. casserole and ½ cup water.
Brussels Sprouts				
Whole	2 to 2½ cups	4 - 5 min.	5 - 7 min.	
Carrots				
Slices, ⅛-in.	2 cups	4½ - 6 min.	4 - 7 min.	
Cauliflower				
Flowerets	2 cups	4 - 4½ min.	4 - 7 min.	Use 1½-qt. casserole and ¼ cup water.
Greens				
Spinach leaves, bite-size pieces	4 to 5 cups	4 - 5 min.	5 - 8 min.	
Swiss chard leaves, bite-size pieces	4 to 5 cups	3½ - 4 min.	5 - 8 min.	
Turnip leaves, bite-size pieces	4 to 5 cups	4½ - 6½ min.	5 - 8 min.	
Peas				
Whole	2 cups	4 - 5 min.	4 - 6 min.	
Squash				
Yellow, Zucchini, slices, ¼-in.	2 cups	3½ - 4 min.	4 - 7 min.	Omit water.

*To blanch, follow photo directions, opposite.

**To microwave frozen blanched vegetables, place in 1-qt. covered casserole with 2 tablespoons water. Stir once. Let stand, covered, 3 to 5 minutes.

Frozen Convenience Vegetable Cooking Chart

Vegetable	Amount	Microwave Time at High	Procedure (Use covered casserole.)
Pouch	6 to 9 oz. 10 oz.	3 - 6 min. 6 - 9 min.	Flex pouch. Cut large "X" in one side. Place cut side down in 1-qt. casserole. Stir before serving.
Box	6 to 9 oz. 10 oz.	3 - 6 min. 6 - 9 min.	1-qt. casserole. 2 tablespoons water. Stir once. Let stand 2 to 3 minutes.
Bag	½ cup 1 cup	1 - 2½ min. 2 - 4 min.	12-oz. casserole. 1 teaspoon water. Stir once. 15- or 22-oz. casserole. 2 teaspoons water. Stir once.

Stuffed Zucchini pictured on page 114

4 medium zucchini
¼ cup chopped green pepper
¼ cup chopped celery
¼ cup chopped onion
1 tablespoon butter or margarine
1 cup uncooked instant rice
1 container frozen Tomato Sauce, defrosted, page 123*

¼ cup water
1 tablespoon snipped fresh parsley
½ teaspoon chili powder
½ teaspoon salt
⅛ teaspoon pepper
½ teaspoon Worcestershire sauce

To serve:
¼ cup dairy sour cream
2 tablespoons chopped black olives

Makes 2 side dishes
4 servings each

*Or use 1 can (8 oz.) tomato sauce plus ¼ teaspoon sugar, ⅛ teaspoon dried basil leaves and ⅛ teaspoon onion powder.

How to Microwave Stuffed Zucchini

Halve zucchini lengthwise. Scoop out pulp leaving ¼-in. shell. Chop pulp coarsely and set aside. Place zucchini shells cut side up on baking sheet. Cover with plastic wrap. Microwave at High 4 to 4½ minutes, or until very hot.

Combine chopped zucchini, green pepper, celery, onion and butter in 2-qt. casserole. Cover. Microwave at High 5 to 8 minutes, or until tender, stirring after half the time.

Stir in rice, tomato sauce, water, parsley, chili powder, salt, pepper and Worcestershire sauce; cover. Microwave at High 4 to 9 minutes, or until liquid is absorbed and rice is tender.

Spoon into zucchini shells. Freeze until firm. Wrap in groups of four. Label and freeze no longer than 2 months.

To serve, unwrap one package and place shells on roasting rack. Cover with wax paper. Microwave at High 5 to 10 minutes, or until hot, rearranging shells once.

Let stand, covered, 5 minutes. Garnish each zucchini half with 1 tablespoon sour cream and 1½ teaspoons olives.

118

Coleslaw

1 medium head green
    cabbage (2 to 2½ lbs.),
    shredded
1 cup shredded carrot
½ medium green pepper, finely
    chopped
2 tablespoons finely chopped
    onion

1 teaspoon salt

Dressing:
1 cup sugar
¾ cup vinegar
½ cup water
½ teaspoon celery seed
    Dash pepper

Makes 3 side dishes
4 servings each

In large bowl combine cabbage, carrot, green pepper, onion and salt. Let stand at least 1 hour. Drain.

While cabbage stands, mix all dressing ingredients in 1-qt. casserole. Microwave at High 4 to 6 minutes, or until boiling, stirring every other minute. Continue to boil 1 minute. Cool slightly. Pour over drained cabbage mixture; toss well. Spoon into three freezer containers. Label and freeze no longer than 2 weeks.

To serve, remove from one container and place in 1-qt. casserole or serving bowl. Microwave at 50% (Medium) 3 to 6 minutes, or until coleslaw can be broken apart but is still very cold and ice crystals remain, breaking up and stirring once during cooking time. Let stand 5 to 10 minutes.

Sweet & Sour Beets

1 lb. beets (5 medium)
½ cup hot water
½ teaspoon salt
1 tablespoon butter or
    margarine

1 tablespoon plus 1½
    teaspoons packed brown
    sugar
1 tablespoon plus 1½
    teaspoons cider vinegar

Serves 4

Leave root ends and 2 inches of tops on beets. Wash gently. Place in 1½-qt. casserole. Mix water and salt until dissolved. Pour over beets. Cover. Microwave at High 14 to 18 minutes, or until fork tender, stirring 1 or 2 times. Let stand, covered, 3 to 5 minutes. Slip off skins and tops. Trim root ends. Slice beets about ¼ inch thick. Place in freezer container.

Place butter in small bowl. Microwave at High 30 to 45 seconds, or until butter melts. Stir in brown sugar and vinegar. Microwave at High 1½ to 3 minutes, or until sugar dissolves, stirring once after half the time. Pour over beets in freezer container. Label and freeze no longer than 1 month.

To serve, remove from container and place in 1-qt. casserole. Cover. Microwave at High 7 to 10 minutes, or until hot, stirring and separating beets after half the cooking time.

◄ Green Beans With Ricotta Garlic Sauce

3 cups frozen green beans
1 container Ricotta Garlic
    Sauce, defrosted, below

Serves 4 to 6

Place green beans in 1-qt. casserole; cover. Microwave at High 4 to 8 minutes, or until tender. Drain. Let stand, covered, while defrosting and heating sauce.

Ricotta Garlic Sauce

1⅓ cups ricotta cheese
 1 cup plain yogurt
 1 small clove garlic
 ¼ teaspoon salt
 2 or 3 drops red pepper
    sauce

Makes 2 cups

In blender or food processor, blend all ingredients until smooth. Spoon into two freezer containers. Label and freeze no longer than 2 months.

To serve, remove sauce from one container and place in bowl. Microwave at 50% (Medium) 4 to 8 minutes, or until heated, breaking apart and stirring 1 or 2 times. Serve over hot cooked green beans.

Eggplant Ricotta ▲

1 container frozen Breaded
    Eggplant Slices, opposite
¾ cup ricotta cheese
½ cup milk
½ teaspoon salt
¼ teaspoon onion powder
½ cup shredded mozzarella
    cheese
1 medium tomato, peeled and
    chopped
2 tablespoons grated
    Parmesan cheese
½ teaspoon dried parsley flakes

Serves 4 to 6

Arrange frozen eggplant slices in single layer in 8 × 8-in. baking dish. Overlap edges if necessary. Cover with wax paper. Microwave at High 2 to 4 minutes, or until defrosted, rearranging slices after half the cooking time.

In small bowl combine ricotta cheese, milk, salt and onion powder. Pour evenly over eggplant. Sprinkle with mozzarella cheese. Cover with wax paper. Reduce power to 50% (Medium). Microwave 5 to 7 minutes, or until cheese melts, rotating dish 1 or 2 times. Sprinkle with tomato, Parmesan cheese and parsley. Re-cover. Microwave at 50% (Medium) 3 to 6 minutes, or until hot.

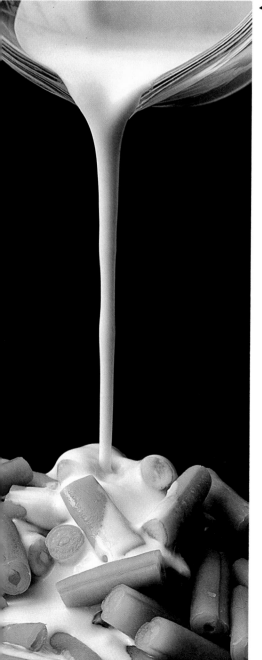

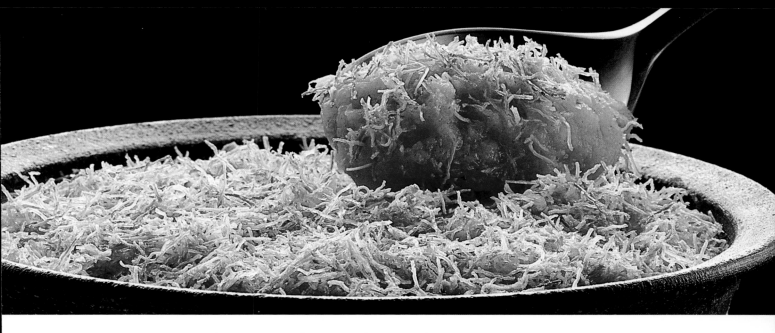

Breaded Eggplant Slices

1 eggplant (1¼ lbs.), peeled
4 cups hot water
1 tablespoon salt
2 tablespoons butter or
   margarine
1 egg, beaten
⅔ cup dry seasoned bread
   crumbs
⅓ cup wheat germ

           Makes 14 to 16 slices

Cut eggplant into ½-in. slices.
Cut slices larger than 4 inches
in diameter in half. Mix water
and salt. Soak eggplant slices
in salt water 5 minutes. Drain.

Melt butter in shallow dish at
High 30 to 45 seconds. Blend in
egg. In another shallow dish,
mix bread crumbs and wheat
germ. Dip eggplant slices in
egg mixture, then coat with
crumbs. Arrange half of slices
around edge of baking sheet.

Microwave at High 8 to 11
minutes, or until just fork tender,
rotating baking sheet twice
during cooking time. Place on
wax paper-lined tray. Repeat
with remaining slices. Freeze
until firm. Package in two
freezer containers. Label and
freeze no longer than 2 months.
Use in Eggplant Ricotta,
opposite, and Ratatouille Pie,
page 123.

Squash Casserole ▲

6 lbs. acorn squash (about 4
   medium)
½ cup butter or margarine, cut
   into pieces
1 can (16 oz.) applesauce
1 tablespoon plus 1 teaspoon
   instant minced onion
1 teaspoon salt
¾ teaspoon ground allspice

Topping:
1 tablespoon plus 1 teaspoon
   butter or margarine
⅔ cup crumbled shredded
   wheat cereal (2 large
   biscuits)
¾ teaspoon salt
5 to 7 drops red pepper sauce

           Makes 2 side dishes
           4 to 6 servings each

Halve each squash lengthwise. Scoop out seeds and fibers. Place
3 pounds of squash on baking sheet; cover with plastic wrap.
Microwave at High 8 to 11 minutes, or until squash is fork tender,
rearranging 1 or 2 times. Let stand 5 minutes. Repeat with
remaining squash.

Scoop squash from skin into large mixing bowl. Blend in butter
with electric mixer until squash is smooth and butter melts. Blend
in applesauce, minced onion, salt and allspice. Spoon into two
freezer containers. Label and freeze no longer than 3 months.

For topping, place butter in small bowl. Microwave at High 30 to
45 seconds, or until butter melts. Stir in cereal, salt and red pepper
sauce. Spoon into two freezer containers. Label and freeze no
longer than 3 months.

To serve, remove squash from one container and place in 1½-qt.
casserole. Cover with wax paper. Microwave at High 10 to 15
minutes, or until hot, breaking apart and stirring 2 or 3 times.
Sprinkle with cereal topping from one container. Microwave at High
1 minute. Let stand 2 minutes.

Twice-Baked Potatoes

4 large baking potatoes,
   scrubbed
¾ cup milk
¼ cup butter or margarine
1 teaspoon salt
⅛ teaspoon pepper
½ cup frozen peas
½ cup shredded carrot
1 tablespoon finely chopped
   onion, optional
1 tablespoon water

To serve:
¼ cup shredded Cheddar
   cheese

Makes 2 side dishes
4 servings each

Pierce potatoes twice with fork. Arrange at least 1 inch apart on paper towel on oven floor. Microwave at High 12 to 18 minutes, or until still slightly firm, rearranging and turning over after half the time. Cover with an inverted casserole; let stand 5 to 10 minutes. Halve each potato lengthwise. Scoop out center. Mash with milk, butter, salt and pepper.

In 1-qt. casserole combine peas, carrot, onion and water; cover. Microwave at High 1½ to 3½ minutes, or until tender. Drain; stir into mashed potatoes. Spoon mixture evenly into shells. Place stuffed shells on wax paper-lined tray. Freeze until firm. Wrap in two packages. Label and freeze no longer than 2 months.

To serve, unwrap one package and place potato halves on serving plate. Cover with wax paper. Microwave at High 8 to 11 minutes, or until hot, rearranging 1 or 2 times. Sprinkle each half with 1 tablespoon cheese. Microwave at High 1 to 2 minutes, or until cheese melts, rotating plate once during cooking time. Let stand 3 minutes.

Ratatouille Pie ▶

2 tablespoons dry seasoned
    bread crumbs
2 small zucchini (½ lb.), cut
    diagonally into ¼-in. slices
2 tablespoons grated
    Parmesan cheese
1 small onion, cut in half, then
    cut into strips
1 medium green pepper,
    chopped
1 clove garlic, minced
1 tablespoon olive oil
1 container frozen Tomato
    Sauce, defrosted, right*
½ teaspoon dried oregano
    leaves
⅛ teaspoon pepper
1 container frozen Breaded
    Eggplant Slices, page 121

Serves 4 to 6

Generously butter 9-in. pie plate. Coat sides and bottom with bread crumbs, leaving any extra crumbs on bottom of plate. Set aside.

Place zucchini in 1-qt. casserole; cover. Microwave at High 2 to 4 minutes, or until tender-crisp, stirring 1 or 2 times. Drain. Layer zucchini in pie plate along sides and bottom. (Layers will overlap). Sprinkle with Parmesan cheese. Set aside.

In medium bowl combine onion, green pepper, garlic and olive oil; cover. Microwave at High 3 to 5 minutes, or until vegetables are tender. Drain. Stir in tomato sauce, oregano and pepper. Spoon over zucchini. Top with frozen eggplant slices. Microwave at High 7 to 12 minutes, or until hot, rotating plate 1 or 2 times. Let stand 2 minutes. Garnish with sliced black olives, if desired.

*Or use 1 can (8 oz.) tomato sauce plus ¼ teaspoon sugar, ⅛ teaspoon dried basil leaves and ⅛ teaspoon onion powder.

Tomato Sauce

3 qts. hot water
12 medium tomatoes
 1 can (12 oz.) tomato paste
¼ cup chopped green pepper
¼ cup chopped onion
 1 tablespoon olive oil

2 teaspoons sugar
1 teaspoon salt
½ teaspoon dried basil leaves
¼ teaspoon pepper
1 bay leaf

Makes six 1-cup servings

Place hot water in 5-qt. casserole; cover. Microwave at High 18 to 25 minutes, or until boiling. Dip half the tomatoes in water. Let stand 30 seconds to 1½ minutes, or until skins begin to loosen. Plunge tomatoes in cold water. Remove skins and core. Cut in half crosswise; remove seeds. Repeat with remaining tomatoes. Purée tomatoes with food processor, blender or by mashing.

In 3-qt. casserole combine purée and all remaining ingredients; cover. Microwave at High 10 minutes. Stir. Microwave, uncovered, at High 35 to 45 minutes, or until sauce is thickened, stirring several times. Cool. Spoon into six freezer containers. Label and freeze no longer than 3 months.

To defrost, remove from one container and place in small bowl or casserole. Microwave at High 2 to 4 minutes, breaking apart and stirring every minute.

Gnocchi

3 lbs. baking potatoes, peeled
4½ cups hot water, divided
2½ teaspoons salt, divided
2 tablespoons butter or margarine
1½ cups all-purpose flour
¾ cup grated Parmesan cheese
3 egg yolks, slightly beaten
¼ teaspoon pepper

Makes 3 side dishes
4 to 6 servings each

How to Microwave Gnocchi

Combine potatoes, ½ cup hot water and ½ teaspoon salt in 3-qt. casserole; cover. Microwave at High 17 to 25 minutes, or until fork tender, stirring 1 or 2 times. Drain.

Mash potatoes with butter. Blend in flour and cheese. Mix in egg yolks, remaining 2 teaspoons salt and pepper. On floured board, shape about ½ cup into ½-in. diameter roll.

Cut roll into 1-in. pieces. Set aside. Repeat with remaining mixture. Place remaining 4 cups water in shallow 3-qt. casserole; cover. Microwave at High 7 to 11 minutes, or until boiling.

Add one-third of gnocchi. Microwave, uncovered, at High 2 to 6 minutes, or until gnocchi begins to float, stirring gently with rubber spatula after 1 minute, then every other minute.

Remove with slotted spoon to paper towel-lined platter to dry. Repeat twice, one-third at a time. If necessary, change water after second batch.

Arrange dry gnocchi on wax paper-lined trays. Freeze until firm. Package in three freezer containers. Label and freeze no longer than 3 months. Use in recipes, opposite.

124

Gnocchi in Tomato Sauce ▲

2 containers frozen Tomato
  Sauce, page 123*
1 container frozen Gnocchi,
  opposite
3 tablespoons grated Parmesan
  cheese
1 tablespoon snipped fresh
  parsley

Serves 4 to 6

Place frozen tomato sauce in
1-qt. bowl; cover. Microwave at
High 2½ to 5 minutes, or until
defrosted and slightly warm,
stirring and breaking sauce
apart every minute.

Add frozen gnocchi to tomato
sauce; cover. Reduce power to
70% (Medium-High). Microwave
9 to 13 minutes, or until heated,
stirring once.

Sprinkle Parmesan cheese and
parsley over top. Microwave,
uncovered, at 70% (Medium-
High) 2½ to 4½ minutes, or until
cheese melts, rotating bowl ½
turn after half the cooking time.

*Or use 1 can (15 oz.) tomato
sauce plus ½ teaspoon sugar,
¼ teaspoon dried basil leaves
and ¼ teaspoon onion powder.

Cheesy Gnocchi ►

¼ cup shredded mozzarella
  cheese
1 tablespoon shredded
  Cheddar cheese
¼ teaspoon paprika
1 tablespoon butter or
  margarine
⅛ teaspoon onion powder
1 container frozen Gnocchi,
  opposite
¼ cup shredded carrot

Serves 4 to 6

In small bowl combine
mozzarella cheese, Cheddar
cheese and paprika. Toss to
coat with paprika. Set aside.
Place butter and onion powder
in 9-in. pie plate. Microwave at
High 30 to 45 seconds, or until
butter melts.

Gently stir frozen gnocchi and
carrot into melted butter until
coated. Cover with wax paper.
Reduce power to 70% (Me-
dium-High). Microwave 5 to 7
minutes, or until heated, gently
stirring once.

Sprinkle cheese mixture over
gnocchi. Microwave, uncovered,
at 70% (Medium-High) 1½ to
3½ minutes, or until melted,
rotating plate ½ turn after half
the cooking time.

Rice

Rice cooked in the microwave oven and stored in the freezer, can be ready to serve in minutes. The vegetable-rice mix is delicious by itself, or as the base for Fried or Curried Rice.

Vegetable-Rice Mix ►

2 cups sliced fresh mushrooms
1 medium carrot, finely
    chopped
½ cup chopped green pepper
½ cup chopped celery
¼ cup chopped onion
1 clove garlic, minced
2 tablespoons butter or
    margarine
4 cups cooked brown or white
    rice, right
½ teaspoon salt
    Dash pepper

> Makes 2 side dishes
> 4 to 6 servings each

In 2-qt. casserole combine mushrooms, carrot, green pepper, celery, onion, garlic and butter; cover. Microwave at High 4 to 5½ minutes, or until vegetables are tender-crisp, stirring after half the cooking time. Stir in rice, salt and pepper. Spoon into two freezer containers. Label and freeze no longer than 1 month.

To defrost, remove from one container and place in 1- to 1½-qt. casserole; cover. Microwave at High 2 minutes. Break apart. Microwave at High 1 to 2 minutes, or until defrosted. To serve, continue to microwave, covered, at High 2 to 4 minutes, or until heated, stirring once.

White Rice

2⅔ cups hot water
1⅓ cups uncooked long grain
    rice
1 tablespoon butter or
    margarine
1 teaspoon salt

> Makes 2 side dishes
> 2 cups each

In 3-qt. casserole combine all ingredients; cover. Microwave at High 5 minutes. Reduce power to 50% (Medium). Microwave 14 to 17 minutes, or until liquid is absorbed and rice is tender. Let stand 5 minutes. Fluff with fork. Spoon into two freezer containers. Label and freeze no longer than 1 month.

To serve, remove from one container and place in 1-qt. casserole; cover. Microwave at High 4 to 8 minutes, or until hot, breaking apart and stirring 2 or 3 times.

Brown Rice ▲

2⅓ cups hot water
1¼ cups uncooked brown rice
1 tablespoon butter or
    margarine
1 teaspoon salt

> Makes 2 side dishes
> 2 cups each

In 3-qt. casserole combine all ingredients; cover. Microwave at High 5 minutes. Reduce power to 50% (Medium). Microwave 30 to 40 minutes, or until liquid is absorbed and rice is tender. Let stand 5 minutes. Fluff with fork. Spoon into two freezer containers. Label and freeze no longer than 1 month.

To serve, remove from one container and place in 1-qt. casserole; cover. Microwave at High 4 to 8 minutes, or until hot, breaking apart and stirring 2 or 3 times.

Wild Rice ▲

1 cup plus 2 tablespoons
   uncooked wild rice
3 cups hot water
1 tablespoon butter or
   margarine, optional
½ teaspoon salt, optional

Makes 2 side dishes
1½ cups each

Rinse rice under cold running water; drain. In 3-qt. casserole combine rice with remaining ingredients; cover. Microwave at High 5 minutes. Reduce power to 50% (Medium). Microwave 18 to 24 minutes, or until rice is tender. Drain. Spoon into two freezer containers. Label and freeze no longer than 1 month.

To serve, remove from one container and place in 1-qt. casserole; cover. Microwave at High 4 to 7 minutes, or until hot, breaking apart and stirring 2 or 3 times during cooking.

Fried Rice ▲

1 container frozen
   Vegetable-Rice Mix,
   defrosted, opposite
2 cups cut-up cooked
   chicken, beef or pork
2 eggs, slightly beaten
1½ teaspoons butter or
   margarine
1 tablespoon soy sauce

Serves 6 to 8

In 1½-qt. casserole combine Vegetable-Rice Mix and meat; cover. Microwave at High 4 to 7 minutes, or until heated, stirring after half the time. Set aside.

Place eggs and butter in small bowl or casserole. Microwave at High 1 to 1¾ minutes, or until eggs are set, stirring after half the cooking time. Chop eggs into small pieces. Stir into rice mixture. Add soy sauce, tossing to coat rice.

Curried Rice ▲

½ cup chopped peeled apple
1 tablespoon butter or
   margarine
1 container frozen Vegetable-
   Rice Mix, defrosted,
   opposite
¼ cup raisins
1 teaspoon curry powder
½ teaspoon sugar
¼ cup cashews

Serves 4 to 6

Place apple and butter in small bowl. Microwave at High 1½ to 3 minutes, or until apple is tender. In 1-qt. casserole mix Vegetable-Rice Mix, apple, raisins, curry powder and sugar; cover. Microwave at High 4½ to 7 minutes, or until heated, stirring once. Mix in cashews.

Breads

Prepare and freeze these special breads ahead and serve them when you have a limited amount of time. To prevent drying, package carefully. Enclose the bread airtight in plastic wrap, then overwrap with heavy-duty foil or freezer paper.

Brandied Apple Loaf ▲

Graham cracker crumbs
¼ cup brandy
2 cups peeled and chopped apple
½ cup raisins
½ cup chopped walnuts
1½ cups all-purpose flour
1½ cups whole wheat flour
¾ teaspoon baking soda
¾ teaspoon baking powder
½ teaspoon salt
¾ cup packed dark brown sugar
½ cup shortening
¾ cup apple juice
2 eggs
¼ cup butter or margarine, softened

Makes 2 loaves

Generously grease two 8 × 5-in. loaf dishes. Coat bottom and sides of each dish with graham cracker crumbs. Place brandy in small bowl. Microwave at High 30 to 45 seconds, or until warm. Stir in apple, raisins and walnuts. Set aside.

In large mixing bowl combine remaining ingredients. Beat at medium speed of electric mixer 3 minutes, or until blended, scraping bowl constantly. Stir in apple mixture. Spread equally in dishes. Shield ends of dishes with foil. Place one loaf at a time in oven on saucer. Microwave at 50% (Medium) 6 minutes. Remove shielding.

Increase power to High. Microwave 2 to 6 minutes, or until top springs back when touched lightly and no unbaked batter appears through bottom of dish. Let stand on counter 5 to 10 minutes. Loosen edges. Invert on wire rack; cool. Wrap each loaf. Label and freeze no longer than 1 month.

To serve, unwrap and place one loaf on plate. Microwave at 50% (Medium) 3½ to 5½ minutes, or until wooden pick can be easily inserted in center. Let stand 5 minutes.

Cinnamon Loaf & Ring Coffee Cake

pictured on page 128 and above

Topping:
⅓ cup packed brown sugar
¼ cup butter or margarine
1 teaspoon ground cinnamon
½ cup chopped walnuts or pecans

Cake:
2¾ cups all-purpose flour
1 cup packed brown sugar
2 teaspoons ground cinnamon
1 teaspoon baking powder
1 teaspoon baking soda
½ teaspoon salt
2 cups buttermilk
½ cup shortening
½ cup honey
¼ cup butter or margarine, softened
2 eggs

To serve each cake:
1 to 2 teaspoons half and half
⅓ cup powdered sugar

Makes 1 loaf coffee cake and 1 ring coffee cake

How to Microwave Loaf Cinnamon Coffee Cake

Line bottom of loaf dish with wax paper. In small bowl combine all topping ingredients except nuts. Microwave at High 1 to 2 minutes, or until mixture is bubbly, stirring 1 or 2 times.

Stir in nuts. Spread half of topping in dish. Reserve remaining topping for ring cake, below. Place all cake ingredients in large mixing bowl. Beat at low speed of electric mixer 30 seconds, scraping bowl constantly.

Beat at medium speed 2 minutes, scraping bowl occasionally. Spread enough batter in prepared loaf dish to fill half full. Reserve remaining batter for ring cake.

Shield ends of dish with foil. Place on saucer in oven. Microwave at 50% (Medium) 6 minutes, rotating 1 or 2 times. Remove shields. Increase power to High.

Microwave 2 to 6 minutes, or until no unbaked batter can be seen through bottom of dish, rotating 1 or 2 times. Let stand on counter 10 minutes. Loosen edges; invert on wire rack. Cool. Wrap, label and freeze no longer than 1 month.

To serve, unwrap and place on plate. Microwave at 50% (Medium) 1½ to 3½ minutes, or until wooden pick can be easily inserted. Let stand 5 minutes. To glaze, stir half and half into powdered sugar until of desired consistency. Drizzle over cake.

How to Microwave Ring Cinnamon Coffee Cake

Line bottom of ring dish with wax paper. Microwave reserved topping at High 30 to 60 seconds; spread in dish. Spread remaining cake batter over topping. Place dish on saucer in oven.

Microwave and rotate as directed for loaf, above, or until top springs back when touched lightly. Let stand on counter 10 minutes. Cool and freeze as directed above.

To serve, defrost ring cake as directed for loaf, except increase microwaving time to 3½ to 5 minutes. Glaze as directed above.

Onion Bread ▲

¼ cup instant minced onion
1 cup hot water
   Cornflake crumbs
2 cups all-purpose flour
1 cup whole wheat flour
1 cup rye flour
¼ cup grated Parmesan
   cheese
3 teaspoons baking powder

1 teaspoon baking soda
½ teaspoon dried oregano
   leaves
½ teaspoon salt
⅛ teaspoon pepper
1 cup buttermilk
⅔ cup vegetable oil
2 eggs, slightly beaten

Makes 2 loaves

In small bowl combine onion and hot water. Set aside. Generously grease two 8 × 5-in. loaf dishes. Coat bottom and sides of each dish with fine cornflake crumbs. In large bowl combine flours, cheese, baking powder, baking soda, oregano, salt and pepper.

In medium bowl mix remaining ingredients. Add with onions and water to dry ingredients, stirring until moistened. Pour half in each loaf dish. Shield ends of dishes with foil. Place one loaf at a time in oven on saucer.

Microwave at 50% (Medium) 6 minutes, rotating every 2 minutes. Remove shields. Increase power to High. Microwave 1½ to 2 minutes, or until top springs back when touched lightly and no unbaked batter appears through bottom of dish. Let stand on counter 10 minutes. Loosen edges. Invert on wire rack; cool. Wrap each loaf. Label and freeze no longer than 1 month.

To serve, unwrap and place one loaf on plate. Microwave at 50% (Medium) 3½ to 5 minutes, or until wooden pick can be easily inserted, rotating 1 or 2 times.

Whole Wheat Blueberry Muffins pictured at right, top

Topping:
2 tablespoons packed brown
   sugar
2 tablespoons granulated
   sugar
½ teaspoon ground cinnamon

Muffins:
1 cup all-purpose flour
1 cup whole wheat flour
⅓ cup packed brown sugar
2 teaspoons baking powder
½ teaspoon grated lemon peel
¼ teaspoon salt
¼ cup butter or margarine
1 cup milk
⅓ cup vegetable oil
2 eggs, slightly beaten
1 can (14 oz.) blueberries,
   rinsed and drained

Makes 18 muffins

Line six custard cups or microwave muffin cups with two paper liners each. In small bowl mix topping ingredients. Set aside. In medium bowl combine flours, brown sugar, baking powder, lemon peel and salt. Place butter in small bowl. Microwave at High 45 to 60 seconds, or until butter melts. Mix butter, milk, oil and eggs into dry ingredients just until particles are moistened. Gently fold in blueberries. Fill cups half full. Arrange in ring if using custard cups.

Microwave at High as directed in chart, opposite, or until tops spring back when touched lightly, sprinkling each with about ½ teaspoon topping after 1 minute, and rotating after half the time. Remove from cups to wire rack. Moist spots will dry during cooling. Repeat with remaining muffins. Wrap, label and freeze no longer than 1 month.

To serve, unwrap desired number of muffins. Microwave at High 15 to 30 seconds per muffin, or until warm to the touch. Let stand 3 minutes.

Pineapple Bran Muffins
pictured at right, middle

Topping:
- 2 tablespoons butter or margarine
- ¼ cup whole bran cereal, crushed
- ¼ cup graham cracker crumbs

Muffins:
- ½ cup milk
- ¼ cup whole bran cereal
- ¾ cup all-purpose flour
- ¾ cup whole wheat flour
- ¾ cup packed dark brown sugar
- 1½ teaspoons baking powder
- 2 cans (8 oz. each) crushed pineapple, drained, ⅓ cup liquid reserved
- ½ cup vegetable oil
- 1 egg, slightly beaten

Makes 18 muffins

Line six custard cups or microwave muffin cups with two paper liners each. Melt butter in small bowl at High 30 to 45 seconds. Stir in ¼ cup cereal and the graham cracker crumbs until coated. Set aside.

In 1-cup measure combine milk and ¼ cup cereal. Let stand 2 to 3 minutes. In medium bowl mix flours, brown sugar and baking powder. Stir in remaining muffin ingredients and bran mixture just until particles are moistened. Fill cups half full. Sprinkle with topping. Arrange in ring if using custard cups.

Microwave at High as directed in chart, right, or until tops spring back when touched lightly, rotating and rearranging after half the time. Remove from cups to wire rack. Moist spots will dry during cooling. Repeat with remaining muffins. Wrap, label and freeze no longer than 1 month.

To serve, unwrap desired number of muffins. Microwave at High 15 to 30 seconds per muffin, or until warm to the touch. Let stand 3 minutes.

Corn Muffins
pictured at right, bottom

- ¼ cup vegetable oil
- ½ cup all-purpose flour
- ½ cup yellow cornmeal
- 1 tablespoon sugar
- 2 teaspoons baking powder
- ½ teaspoon salt
- 1 egg
- ⅓ cup milk

Makes 6 to 8 muffins

Line six custard cups or microwave muffin cups with two paper liners each. In medium bowl mix all ingredients just until particles are moistened. Fill cups half full. Arrange in ring if using custard cups.

Microwave at High as directed in chart, below, or until tops spring back when touched lightly, rotating once. Remove from cups to wire rack. Moist spots will dry during cooling. Repeat with any remaining muffins. Wrap, label and freeze no longer than 1 month.

To serve, unwrap desired number of muffins. Microwave at High 15 to 30 seconds per muffin, or until warm to the touch. Let stand 3 minutes.

Amount	Microwave Time at High
1 muffin	20 - 40 seconds
2 muffins	½ - 1½ minutes
4 muffins	1 - 2½ minutes
6 muffins	2 - 4½ minutes

Freezing Desserts

By using the microwave oven and freezer you can quickly serve glamorous desserts for entertaining or family meals. For a quick light dessert or snack, microwave a plate of cookies in 1 to 4 minutes. Even when frozen, cakes and pies are delicate. Choose a place in the freezer where they will not be damaged by contact with hard or sharp objects.

How to Freeze Cakes

Freeze frosted cakes until firm before wrapping to avoid marring the frosting.

Wrap airtight in plastic wrap. Overwrap with heavy-duty foil.

Underwrap unfrosted cakes as soon as they are cool to prevent drying. Overwrap.

How to Freeze Pies

Use glass or ovenable paper pie plates to prepare, freeze and defrost pies.

Leave pie in pie plate and place in freezer until firm.

Wrap pie and plate airtight in heavy-duty foil.

How to Freeze & Serve Molded Desserts

Freeze molded desserts in their dishes. Wrap securely with heavy-duty foil.

To serve, unwrap and dip briefly in hot water.

Loosen edges of mold with knife. Invert onto serving plate.

Defrosting Frozen Convenience Dessert Chart

Item	Package Weight	Defrost Time at 30% (Medium-Low)	Procedure
Layer Cake with icing	10 to 13¾ oz. 15¾ to 18 oz. 21 to 24 oz.	1 - 3½ min. 1½ - 4 min. 3½ - 6 min.	Remove from box. Transfer one-layer cake from foil pan to serving plate. Two- and three-layer cakes can be defrosted on styrofoam base or serving plate. Defrost until wooden pick can be easily inserted in center, rotating 2 or 3 times. Let stand 15 to 20 minutes.
Pound Cake	9½ to 12⅞ oz. 16 oz.	¾ - 1½ min. 1 - 2 min.	Remove from box. Transfer to serving plate. Defrost until wooden pick can be easily inserted in center, rotating 2 or 3 times. Let stand 5 minutes.
Cheesecake	10 oz. 17 to 19 oz.	1 - 3½ min. 1½ - 4 min.	Remove from box. Transfer to serving plate. Defrost until wooden pick can be easily inserted in center, rotating 2 or 3 times. Let stand 10 to 15 minutes.
Brownies	13 oz.	1 - 3 min.	Remove from box. Transfer to paper towel-lined plate. Defrost until wooden pick can be easily inserted in center, rotating 2 or 3 times. Let stand 5 minutes.
Cream Pie	14 oz.	¾ - 2 min.	Remove from box. Transfer to glass pie plate. Defrost until wooden pick can be easily inserted in center, rotating 2 or 3 times. Let stand 5 minutes.
Coffee Cake	6½ to 15 oz.	50% (Med.): 1 - 4 min.	Remove from box. Transfer to paper towel-lined plate. Defrost until wooden pick can be easily inserted in center, rotating 2 or 3 times. Let stand 5 minutes.
Double Crust Pie	26 to 40 oz.	50% (Med.): 5½ - 9 min./lb.	Remove from box. Transfer to glass pie plate. Defrost until wooden pick can be easily inserted in center, rotating after half the time. Bake conventionally as directed on package for one-third to one-half the suggested time.
Pie Crust	5 to 6 oz.	50% (Med.): 30 - 60 sec. High: 2 - 3½ min.	Remove from box. Transfer to glass pie plate. Defrost at 50% (Medium). Form crust to shape of pie plate. Crimp edges; prick with fork at bend of plate, sides and bottom. If adding sweet filling, brush defrosted crust with vanilla. Microwave at High until crust is dry and opaque, rotating after half the time. Fill. If adding a liquid filling, brush microwaved crust with slightly beaten egg yolk. Microwave at High 30 to 60 seconds, or until egg is set. Fill.

Cream-Filled Chocolate Cake

Topping:
- ¼ cup butter or margarine
- 1 cup graham cracker crumbs
- ½ cup chopped nuts

Cake:
- 2 squares (1 oz. each) semi-sweet chocolate
- 1¾ cups all-purpose flour
- 1¼ cups sugar
- 1 teaspoon baking soda
- 1 teaspoon salt
- 4 eggs
- ¾ cup buttermilk
- ⅔ cup shortening
- 1 teaspoon vanilla

Glaze:
- 4 squares (1 oz. each) semi-sweet chocolate
- 1 tablespoon shortening

To serve:
- 1½ cups chilled whipping cream
- 3 tablespoons powdered sugar
- 1 teaspoon vanilla

Makes one 2-layer cake

How to Microwave Cream-Filled Chocolate Cake

Place butter in small bowl. Microwave at High 45 to 60 seconds, or until butter melts. Stir in graham cracker crumbs. Microwave at High 1 minute, stirring after half the time. Mix in nuts. Set aside. To prepare cake, line bottoms of two 9-in. round cake dishes with wax paper circles.

Place two squares of chocolate in small bowl. Microwave at 50% (Medium) 2 to 5 minutes, or until smooth when stirred. Set aside. Combine all cake ingredients except chocolate in large bowl. Blend at low speed of electric mixer 30 seconds, scraping bowl constantly. Beat at medium speed 2 minutes, scraping occasionally. Stir chocolate well; blend into batter.

Spread half of batter in each dish. Microwave one layer at a time at 50% (Medium) 6 minutes, rotating ¼ turn once. Sprinkle with half of topping. Increase power to High. Microwave 2 to 5 minutes, or until top springs back when lightly touched, rotating 1 or 2 times. Let stand directly on counter 5 to 10 minutes. Remove from dishes. Repeat with remaining layer. Cool on wire rack.

Combine four squares chocolate and 1 tablespoon shortening in 2-cup measure. Microwave at 50% (Medium) 2½ to 6½ minutes, or until chocolate is soft and shiny. Stir well. Drizzle half of glaze over top of each cake layer. Freeze on wire rack just until firm. Wrap separately, label and freeze no longer than 3 months.

To serve, unwrap and place one layer on serving plate. Microwave at 50% (Medium) 3 to 5 minutes, or until wooden pick can be easily inserted in center, rotating plate every other minute. Repeat, placing other layer on paper towel-lined plate. Let layers stand 10 to 15 minutes, or until defrosted but still cold.

Beat whipping cream, powdered sugar and vanilla in chilled bowl until stiff. Spread two-thirds on cake layer on serving plate. Top with remaining layer. Using pastry tube, decorate top of second layer with remaining whipped cream.

Pineapple-Coconut Cake

Cake:

- 1 pkg. (18½ oz.) yellow cake mix
- 2 cans (8¼ oz. each) crushed pineapple
- 3 eggs
- ⅓ cup vegetable oil
- 1 cup shredded coconut

Frosting:

- 1 cup shredded coconut
- ¼ cup butter or margarine
- 4 cups powdered sugar
- 2 to 3 tablespoons rum or half and half
- 1 teaspoon vanilla

Makes two 8 × 8-in. cakes

How to Microwave Pineapple-Coconut Cake

Line bottoms and sides of two 8 × 8-in. cake dishes with double wax paper, extending beyond edge. Place all cake ingredients except coconut in large bowl. Blend at low speed 30 seconds, scraping bowl constantly.

Beat at medium speed 2 minutes, scraping occasionally. Stir in 1 cup coconut. Spread half of batter in each dish. Place one dish on saucer in oven. Microwave at 50% (Medium) 6 minutes, rotating ¼ turn once.

Increase power to High. Microwave 3 to 6 minutes, or until top springs back when lightly touched and no unbaked batter appears through bottom of dish.

Let stand directly on counter 5 to 10 minutes. Cool in dish on wire rack. Repeat with other layer. Spread 1 cup coconut on paper plate. Microwave at High 1½ to 3 minutes, or until toasted, stirring 2 or 3 times.

Place butter in medium bowl. Reduce power to 50% (Medium). Microwave 10 to 15 seconds, or until butter softens.

Add powdered sugar, 2 tablespoons rum and the vanilla. Beat until smooth and of spreading consistency, adding 1 tablespoon rum, a few drops at a time, if necessary.

Frost tops of cooled cakes. Sprinkle each with half of the toasted coconut. Remove from cake dish by gently lifting wax paper. Freeze on wire rack until firm. Wrap separately, label and freeze no longer than 1 month.

To serve, unwrap one cake and place on plate. Microwave at 30% (Medium-Low) 5½ to 8½ minutes, or until wooden pick can be easily inserted in center and frosting softens but does not melt, rotating plate ¼ turn every minute. Let stand 10 to 15 minutes.

Dark Fruitcake

1 pkg. (15 oz.) golden raisins
1 pkg. (8 oz.) dried apricots,
  quartered
⅓ cup brandy
  Graham cracker crumbs
3 cups all-purpose flour
⅔ cup granulated sugar
⅔ cup packed dark brown
  sugar
2 teaspoons ground cinnamon
1 teaspoon baking soda
1 teaspoon salt
½ teaspoon ground nutmeg

¼ teaspoon ground cloves
1⅓ cups shortening
8 eggs
¾ cup orange juice
¼ cup dark molasses
1 pkg. (8 oz.) pitted dates,
  halved
1 cup candied red cherries,
  halved
1 cup candied green
  cherries, halved
2 cups broken pecans
  Brandy

Makes 2 loaves and 1 ring cake

Place raisins and apricots in medium bowl. Pour ⅓ cup brandy into 1-cup measure. Microwave at High 15 to 45 seconds, or until heated. Pour over raisins and apricots. Set aside. Grease two 8×4- or 9×5-in. loaf dishes and one 8-cup ring cake dish. Coat with graham cracker crumbs.

Place remaining ingredients except fruits, pecans and brandy in large bowl. Blend at low speed of electric mixer 30 seconds, scraping bowl constantly. Beat at medium speed 3 minutes, scraping occasionally. Fold in fruits and pecans. Spoon 3¼ cups batter into each loaf dish and remaining batter into ring cake dish. Spread evenly. Shield ends of loaf dishes with foil.

Microwave one loaf dish at a time. Center dish on saucer in oven. Microwave at 50% (Medium) 10 minutes, rotating ¼ turn every 3 to 4 minutes. Remove shields. Increase power to High. Microwave 3½ to 9½ minutes, or until top springs back when lightly touched and no unbaked batter appears through bottom of dish, rotating 1 or 2 times. Let stand directly on counter 5 to 10 minutes. Remove from loaf dish. Cool on wire rack. Repeat with second loaf dish.

Microwave ring cake dish at 50% (Medium) 18 to 25 minutes, or until top springs back when lightly touched and no unbaked batter appears on side, rotating ½ turn every 3 minutes. Let stand directly on counter 5 to 10 minutes. Remove from dish. Cool on wire rack.

Brush all cakes with brandy. Wrap in brandy-moistened cheesecloth. Overwrap with plastic bag or foil. Refrigerate 2 to 3 days to mellow and blend flavors. Remoisten cheesecloth with brandy as needed. Wrap, label and freeze no longer than 6 months.

To serve loaf fruitcake, unwrap one loaf and place on plate. Microwave at 50% (Medium) 3½ to 5½ minutes. Repeat, as desired. To serve ring fruitcake, unwrap and place on plate. Microwave at 50% (Medium) 5½ to 8 minutes, rotating ¼ turn every minute. Fruitcake will still be slightly frozen. Slice carefully.

Rhubarb-Raspberry Pie ▶

1 microwaved 9-in. pie shell,
   right
1 egg yolk, beaten
¼ cup hot water
2 teaspoons unflavored gelatin
4 cups cut-up rhubarb or
   1 pkg. (16 oz.) frozen
   rhubarb
⅔ cup sugar
1 pkg. (10 oz.) frozen
   raspberries
¼ cup butter or margarine
½ cup all-purpose flour
¼ cup packed brown sugar
2 tablespoons quick-cooking
   oats
¼ teaspoon ground nutmeg

Makes one 9-in. pie

Prepare pie shell as directed.
Brush with egg yolk. Microwave
at High 30 to 60 seconds, or
until egg is set. Set aside. Place
water in 1-cup measure. Microwave at High 30 to 60 seconds,
or until boiling. Sprinkle gelatin
over boiling water. Stir until
dissolved. Set aside.

Combine rhubarb and sugar.
Microwave at High 8 to 12
minutes, or until rhubarb is just
tender, stirring 1 or 2 times.
Add raspberries; stir to defrost.
Stir in gelatin mixture. Pour into
pie shell. Cool.

In small bowl cut butter into
flour, brown sugar, oats and
nutmeg with pastry blender.
Sprinkle over pie. Freeze until
firm. Wrap, label and freeze no
longer than 3 months.

To serve, unwrap and microwave at 30% (Medium-Low) 6
to 11½ minutes, or until wooden
pick can be easily inserted in
center, rotating 2 or 3 times,
taking care not to melt edge.
Let stand 10 to 20 minutes.

One Crust Pastry Shell

⅓ cup shortening
2 tablespoons butter or
   margarine, softened
1 cup all-purpose flour
½ teaspoon salt
2 to 4 tablespoons cold water
3 or 4 drops yellow food
   coloring, optional

Makes one 8-, 9- or 10-in. pie shell

Cut shortening and butter into flour and salt using pastry blender
until particles resemble coarse crumbs or small peas. Combine
water and food coloring. Sprinkle over flour mixture while stirring
with fork, until particles are just moist enough to cling together.

Form dough into ball. Flatten ball to ½ inch on lightly floured board
or pastry cloth. Roll out to circle, at least 2 inches larger than
inverted pie plate. Carefully fit into plate, being careful not to
stretch dough. Let stand 10 minutes. Trim pastry overhang to
generous ½ inch. Fold to form high-standing rim; flute. Prick pastry
continuously with fork at bend of plate and ½ inch apart on bottom
and side.

Microwave at High 5 to 7 minutes, rotating plate ½ turn every 3
minutes. If crust cooks unevenly, rotate ¼ turn every minute. If
brown spot appears, cover with small piece of foil. If crust
bubbles, gently push back into shape. Check for doneness by
looking through bottom of pie plate. Crust will not brown, but will
appear dry and opaque. Cool completely before filling.

Variations:
Whole Wheat: Substitute ½ cup whole wheat flour for ½ cup of
the all-purpose flour. Omit food coloring. Prepare as directed.

Cornmeal: Substitute ⅓ cup yellow cornmeal for ¼ cup of the
all-purpose flour. Omit butter and food coloring. Mix ¼ teaspoon
paprika with the flour, cornmeal and salt. Prepare as directed,
except check for doneness after 3½ minutes.

Graham Cracker Crust

¼ cup plus 1 tablespoon
    butter or margarine
1⅓ cups fine graham cracker or
    cereal crumbs
2 tablespoons granulated
    sugar or packed
    brown sugar

Makes one 9- or
10-in. pie crust

Melt butter in 9- or 10-in. pie
plate at High 45 to 60 seconds.
Stir in crumbs and sugar.
Reserve 2 tablespoons crumb
mixture for garnish, if desired.

Press crumbs firmly and evenly
against bottom and side of
plate, using a smaller pie plate
or custard cup. Microwave at
High 1½ minutes, rotating ½
turn after 1 minute. Cool.

Chocolate-Almond Pie

2 microwaved 9-in. graham
    cracker crusts, left
1 can (12 oz.) almond filling
1 qt. vanilla ice cream
¼ cup Amaretto

½ cup chocolate syrup
2½ cups sweetened whipped
    cream or prepared
    whipped topping

Makes two 9-in. pies

Prepare crusts as directed. Gently spread half of almond filling in
each crust. Set aside. Microwave ice cream at 50% (Medium) 20
to 30 seconds, or until softened. In mixing bowl beat ice cream
and Amaretto with electric mixer just until blended. Divide equally
between two crusts. Freeze 1 hour.

Blend syrup into whipped cream. Spread half on each pie to
cover. Sprinkle with reserved graham cracker crumbs, if desired.
Freeze until firm. Wrap, label and freeze no longer than 1 month.

To serve, unwrap and dip one pie plate at a time in hot water for
about 15 seconds. Microwave at 30% (Medium-Low) 30 to 60
seconds, or until pie is softened, if desired. Store any leftovers in
the freezer.

Chocolate Fudge Pie

- 1 microwaved 9-in. graham cracker crust, opposite
- ½ cup sugar
- 2 tablespoons cornstarch
- ½ teaspoon salt
- 1¾ cups milk
- 4 egg yolks or 2 whole eggs, beaten
- 1 pkg. (6 oz.) semi-sweet chocolate chips
- ½ teaspoon vanilla
- 3 tablespoons coffee liqueur
- 1 cup sweetened whipped cream or prepared whipped topping

Makes one 9-in. pie

Prepare crust as directed. In medium bowl mix sugar, cornstarch and salt. Blend in milk. Microwave at High 6 to 8 minutes, or until thick, stirring 1 or 2 times with wire whip. Stir a small amount of hot mixture into egg yolks. Return to hot mixture, stirring constantly.

Microwave at High 1 to 1½ minutes, or until very thick, blending with wire whip 1 or 2 times. Stir in chocolate chips and vanilla until chips melt. Pour into crust. Chill until set.

Blend liqueur into whipped topping. Spread on cooled filling. Sprinkle with reserved graham cracker crumbs, if desired. Freeze until firm. Wrap, label and freeze no longer than 2 weeks.

To serve, unwrap and dip pie plate in hot water for 15 seconds. Microwave at 30% (Medium-Low) 3 to 6½ minutes, or until wooden pick can be easily inserted in center, rotating 2 or 3 times. Let stand 15 minutes. Store any leftovers in the freezer.

NOTE: If desired, freeze pie without whipped topping. Add just before serving.

Lemon-Blueberry Dessert

pictured at right

3 eggs, separated
½ cup sugar, divided
1 tablespoon grated lemon peel
¼ cup lemon juice
⅓ cup butter or margarine
2½ cups graham cracker crumbs, divided
1 can (21 oz.) blueberry pie filling
2 cups sweetened whipped cream or prepared whipped topping

Makes two 9-in. desserts

Variation:
Double Lemon Dessert:
Substitute 1 can (21 oz.) lemon pie filling for blueberry filling.

Apricot Ring   pictured on page 134

1 can (16 oz.) apricots, drained and 3 tablespoons juice reserved
3 eggs, separated
½ cup sugar
Dash salt
¼ cup apricot preserves

2 tablespoons lemon juice
2 cups sweetened whipped cream or prepared whipped topping

To serve:
1 can (8 oz.) apricots, drained

Serves 6 to 8

Purée apricots in blender or food processor. Set aside. In medium bowl beat egg yolks, sugar and salt until thick and lemon-colored. Blend in preserves, lemon juice and reserved apricot juice. Microwave at 50% (Medium) 5 to 7 minutes, or until thick, stirring 1 or 2 times. Mix in puréed apricots. Cool.

Beat egg whites until stiff peaks form. Fold apricot mixture into egg whites, then fold into whipped cream. Pour into 8-cup ring mold. Wrap, label and freeze no longer than 1 month.

To serve, unwrap and dip mold into hot water for 15 to 30 seconds. Loosen edges with knife. Unmold on plate. Garnish with apricots.

How to Microwave Lemon-Blueberry Dessert

Blend egg yolks, ¼ cup sugar, lemon peel and lemon juice in small bowl. Microwave at 50% (Medium) 3 to 5 minutes, or until thick, stirring 2 or 3 times during cooking. Cool.

Line two 9-in. round cake dishes with foil. Place butter in medium bowl. Microwave at High 45 to 60 seconds, or until butter melts. Stir in 2 cups crumbs until moist.

Press half of crumbs evenly and firmly in bottom of each prepared dish. Gently spoon half of pie filling into each crust, taking care not to lift crumbs. Set aside.

Beat egg whites until foamy. Beat in remaining ¼ cup sugar, 1 tablespoon at a time, until soft peaks form. Fold whipped cream into cooled lemon mixture, then fold into beaten egg whites.

Spread half over pie filling in each dish. Sprinkle each with remaining ½ cup graham cracker crumbs. Freeze until firm. Remove from dishes with foil liner. Wrap, label and freeze no longer than 2 weeks.

To serve, unwrap one package and place in 9-in. round cake dish. Microwave at 30% (Medium-Low) 1½ to 3½ minutes, or until wooden pick can be easily inserted in center, taking care not to melt edge. Let stand 10 to 15 minutes.

◄ Slice & Bake Peanut Butter Cookies

1 cup packed brown sugar
1 cup chunky peanut butter
¼ cup shortening
2 eggs
½ teaspoon baking soda
¼ teaspoon salt
½ teaspoon vanilla
2 cups all-purpose flour
½ cup chopped salted peanuts

Makes 6 dozen

In large bowl mix brown sugar, peanut butter, shortening, eggs, baking soda, salt and vanilla until light and fluffy. Stir in flour and peanuts. Divide dough into three equal parts. Shape each part into roll 6 inches long. (Shaping is made easier by using wax paper.) Wrap each roll in plastic wrap, then in foil or plastic bag. Label and freeze no longer than 3 months.

To serve, unwrap roll and cut into ¼-in. slices. Place six to eight slices in large ring on wax paper-lined baking sheet. Place one or two in center. Microwave at 50% (Medium) 1 to 4 minutes, or just until dry on surface, rotating ¼ turn after 1 minute, then every 30 seconds. Cool cookies on wax paper on counter. Repeat, as desired.

Slice & Bake Whole Wheat Chocolate Chip Cookies ▲

1½ cups packed brown sugar
1½ teaspoons baking soda
½ teaspoon salt
¾ cup butter or margarine
2 eggs
1½ teaspoons vanilla
2 cups all-purpose flour
1½ cups whole wheat flour
1½ cups semi-sweet chocolate chips

Makes 7 to 8 dozen

In large bowl mix brown sugar, baking soda, salt, butter, eggs and vanilla until light and fluffy. Stir in remaining ingredients. Divide dough into four equal parts. Shape each part into roll 6 inches long. (Shaping is made easier by using wax paper.) Wrap each roll in plastic wrap, then in foil or plastic bag. Label and freeze no longer than 3 months.

To serve, unwrap roll and cut into 1-in. slices. Cut each slice into quarters. Place eight quarters in large ring on wax paper-lined baking sheet. Place one or two in center. Microwave at 50% (Medium) 1 to 3½ minutes, or just until dry on surface, rotating ¼ turn after 1 minute, then every 30 seconds. Cool cookies on wax paper on counter. Repeat, as desired.

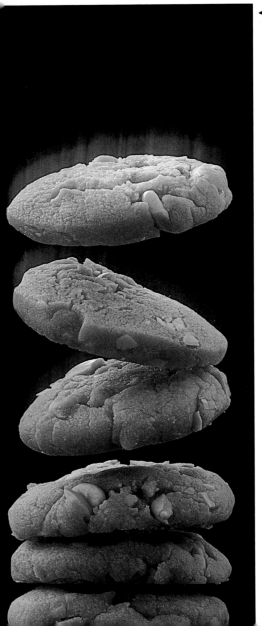

Bread Pudding ▲

½ cup packed brown sugar
2 tablespoons cornstarch
Dash salt
1¾ cups milk
3 eggs
3½ cups whole wheat bread
    cubes, ½-in.
½ cup raisins
½ teaspoon ground cinnamon
¼ teaspoon ground nutmeg

Serves 4 to 6

Line 1½-qt. casserole with foil. In medium bowl blend brown sugar, cornstarch, salt, milk and eggs. In prepared casserole combine bread cubes, raisins, cinnamon and nutmeg, tossing to coat. Pour milk mixture over all. Gently press bread cubes down to moisten. Freeze until firm. Remove from casserole with foil liner. Wrap, label and freeze no longer than 1 month.

To serve, unwrap and place in 1½-qt. casserole. Cover with wax paper. Microwave at 50% (Medium) 25 to 35 minutes, or until soft set in center, gently breaking up and pushing edges toward center with rubber spatula 1 or 2 times. Let stand 10 to 15 minutes.

Cream-Filled Lady Fingers

3 eggs
¼ cup plus 1 tablespoon
    sugar, divided
3 tablespoons hot water
2 teaspoons unflavored gelatin
1 cup chilled whipping cream
1 teaspoon vanilla

36 lady fingers, split
¾ cup semi-sweet chocolate
    chips
2 tablespoons milk
1 tablespoon butter or
    margarine

Makes 3 dozen

Beat eggs at high speed of electric mixer 8 minutes. Beat in 2 tablespoons sugar. Continue beating about 20 minutes, or until mixture reaches consistency of mayonnaise. Beat in additional 2 tablespoons sugar. Refrigerate.

Place water in 1-cup measure. Microwave at High 30 to 60 seconds, or until boiling. Sprinkle gelatin over boiling water. Stir until dissolved. Set aside.

With electric mixer at high speed, blend gelatin mixture into chilled egg mixture. Beat whipping cream and remaining 1 tablespoon sugar until soft peaks form. Stir in vanilla. Fold egg mixture into whipped cream. Refrigerate until chilled. Place one-third to one-half split lady fingers on wax paper-lined tray. Quickly place one-third to one-half of chilled cream mixture in pastry bag with number 6 star tip. (Refrigerate remaining cream mixture until needed.) Squeeze onto bottom of lady fingers. Cover with top of lady fingers. Freeze. Repeat with remaining lady fingers and cream mixture. Freeze 1 hour.

In small bowl combine chips, milk and butter. Microwave at High 1 to 2½ minutes, or until butter melts. Stir to blend. Drizzle over lady fingers. Freeze until firm. Package in freezer containers with wax paper between layers. Label and freeze no longer than 1 month.

To serve, remove 12 lady fingers from container and place on plate. Microwave at 30% (Medium-Low) 1 minute, rotating plate 1 or 2 times. Let stand 5 to 10 minutes at room temperature or in refrigerator 20 to 25 minutes. Repeat, as desired.

Candies

Your microwave oven greatly simplifies the making of cooked candies. Microwaved candies require less attention since they do not need constant stirring. Most of these candies keep well in the freezer for up to six months, so you can take the time to make them pretty and still cut down on the last-minute rush of preparing for the holidays or an important party. Keep a supply of candies on hand year-round to defrost quickly and serve when guests drop in.

◄ Peanut Brittle

3 cups sugar
1½ cups light corn syrup
¼ teaspoon salt
4 cups shelled salted roasted peanuts
3 tablespoons butter or margarine
2 teaspoons vanilla
1 tablespoon baking soda

Makes 3 pounds

Generously butter two large baking sheets. In 3-qt. bowl mix sugar, syrup and salt. Microwave at High 15 minutes, stirring 1 or 2 times. Stir in peanuts. Microwave at High 10 to 15 minutes, or until syrup and peanuts are light brown, stirring after 2 and 4 minutes.

Stir in butter and vanilla until butter melts. Stir in baking soda until light and foamy. Pour half onto each baking sheet and spread quickly to ¼-in. thickness. Cool. Break into pieces. Freeze in single layer on trays until firm. Wrap, label and freeze no longer than 6 months.

To serve, unwrap and arrange in single layer on plate or tray. Let stand at room temperature 15 to 20 minutes.

Cream Cheese Mints

1 pkg. (8 oz.) cream cheese
2 tablespoons butter or margarine
¾ teaspoon mint or wintergreen extract
6 to 7 cups powdered sugar
3 drops food coloring (any color)

Makes 7 to 8 dozen

Place cream cheese in large bowl. Microwave at 50% (Medium) 1 minute to soften. Add butter. Blend in extract. With electric mixer beat in sugar until mixture is very stiff. Blend food coloring into candy. (If desired, divide candy into three parts and blend one drop of a different color into each. One-third could also be left white.)

With pastry bag and number 6 star tip, press mints, 1 to 1½ inches in diameter, onto wax paper-lined baking sheet (if using different colors, wash pastry tube after each color). Let stand at room temperature 24 hours. Freeze in single layer on baking sheet until firm. Wrap, label and freeze no longer than 1 month.

To serve, unwrap and arrange in single layer on plate. Let stand at room temperature 5 to 10 minutes.

◄ Truffles

3 bars (4 oz. each) sweet
    cooking chocolate
¾ cup butter or margarine, cut
    into pieces
2 eggs, beaten
2 egg yolks, beaten
1¾ cups ground filberts,
    divided
⅓ cup white crème de menthe
2 tablespoons cocoa

Makes 3½ to 4½ dozen

Place chocolate in medium
bowl. Microwave at 50%
(Medium) 2 to 5 minutes, or
until melted, stirring 2 or 3
times. Stir in butter until melted.
Blend in eggs and egg yolks.

Microwave at 50% (Medium)
4½ to 5½ minutes, or until very
hot and thickened, stirring with
wire whip several times. Blend
in 1 cup ground filberts and
crème de menthe. Refrigerate 3
hours, or until mixture is firm
enough to shape into balls.
Shape into 1- to 1½-in. balls.

Mix remaining ¾ cup filberts
and the cocoa. Roll balls in
filbert mixture to coat. Freeze in
single layer on tray until firm.
Wrap, label and freeze no
longer than 6 months.

To serve, unwrap 12 truffles
and arrange in single layer on
plate. Microwave at 30%
(Medium-Low) 1 minute,
rearranging once. Let stand 10
minutes. Repeat, as desired.

Praline Fudge ▲

2 cups sugar
1 teaspoon baking soda
1 cup evaporated milk
¾ cup butter or margarine
1 teaspoon vanilla
2 cups milk chocolate or semi-
    sweet chocolate chips
2 cups coarsely broken
    pecans

Makes 3 pounds

Line 10 × 6- or 12 × 8-in. baking
dish with foil. In 3-qt. bowl mix
sugar, baking soda, evaporated
milk and butter. Microwave at
70% (Medium-High) 22 to 27
minutes, or until syrup dropped
into very cold water forms a soft
ball which flattens on removal
from water. Stir several times
during cooking.

Add vanilla. Beat 2 minutes at
high speed of electric mixer,
scraping bowl occasionally.
Add chocolate chips. Beat with
electric mixer until chips melt.
Stir in pecans. Press into
prepared baking dish. Refrigerate until set. Remove from dish
with foil lining. Cut into serving
pieces, but do not separate.
Divide into three 1-pound
sections. Wrap, label and freeze
no longer than 6 months.

To serve, unwrap one package;
separate pieces on plate. Microwave at 30% (Medium-Low) 2
minutes, rearranging every 30
seconds. Let stand 5 to 10
minutes. Repeat, as desired.

Peanut Butter Cups

¾ cup butter or margarine
¾ cup crunchy peanut butter
1½ cups graham cracker
    crumbs
1½ cups powdered sugar
1½ cups milk chocolate chips
3 tablespoons shortening
24 paper nut cups, 1¾ × 1¼-in.

Makes 2 dozen

How to Microwave Peanut Butter Cups

Combine butter and peanut butter in medium bowl. Microwave at 50% (Medium) 2 to 4 minutes, or until butter melts, stirring 1 or 2 times. Stir in crumbs and sugar. Set aside.

Combine chocolate chips and shortening in small bowl. Microwave at 50% (Medium) 1½ to 3 minutes, or until melted, stirring 1 or 2 times.

Place bowl in container of hot water or microwave as necessary at 50% (Medium) 30 seconds to 1½ minutes to keep chocolate from hardening.

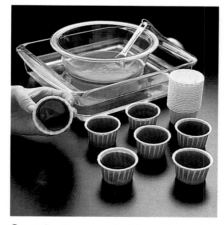

Coat bottom and sides of each paper cup with 1 to 1½ teaspoons chocolate. Let stand until chocolate hardens.

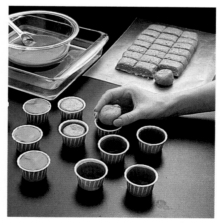

Press peanut butter mixture into each cup. Coat top with chocolate. Freeze in single layer on tray until firm. Wrap, label and freeze no longer than 6 months.

To serve, unwrap 12 and remove nut cups; place on plate in circle. Microwave at 30% (Medium-Low) 3 minutes, rearranging 2 times. Let stand 10 minutes. Repeat, as desired.

Index